Step Out

Advance Praise

"Carolyn Hardy's personal story, illuminated with real life struggles and successes, is inspiration for anyone who dreams of their own business or has already taken the leap. Faced with a storm by changing economic realities and a real-life tornado, she offers the lessons for balancing aspiration and assessment and creating a culture to drive growth and success. As her book title says, it is indeed about stepping up and taking bold moves."

—J. R. "Pitt" Hyde III, Founder AutoZone

"Carolyn Hardy's book has great advice for budding entrepreneurs and for those who have already started their businesses. Much of what she writes reminds me of two key discoveries my dad, Kemmons Wilson, uncovered in his business career. He would have loved to have had the advice Carolyn offers before he started Holiday Inns and Holiday Inn Club Vacations. He was a man of action---'Ready...Fire...Aim' was his mantra. And one of his Twenty Tips is an important reminder to all----'Remember that success requires half luck and half brains.' Thank you, Carolyn, for sharing your discoveries in your book."

—Spence Wilson, Sr., Chairman, Kemmons Wilson Companies, Chairman, Holiday Inn Club Vacations

"As an entrepreneur by trade, bold moves and big ideas can be the difference between success and failure. *Step Out* not only stresses the importance of enterprise leadership, it also provides an up front and honest blueprint on solving some of the most complex business problems alongside your most important asset—your people."

—**Randy Boyd, President,** University of Tennessee System, Founder/Chairman, Radio Systems Corporation

"*Step Out* is a must-have resource for those interested in pursuing entrepreneurial business interests or expanding an existing business. You no longer have to use your best guess or intuition to navigate the challenges associated with starting a new business alone. *Step Out* provides a playbook from the perspective of an experienced, savvy and successful entrepreneur to help identify and address issues you are sure to confront. It's a great read and an affordable investment that can deliver rich returns."

—**Beverly Robertson**, President/CEO, Greater Memphis Chamber of Commerce

"The overwhelming majority of minority-owned businesses are first-generation firms born from the passion of the owner and pure entrepreneurial grit. At the MMBC Continuum, we've found business owners embrace growth strategies presented by minority entrepreneurs that have survived the challenges of business ownership and experienced a level of success. Carolyn Hardy's *Step Out: Bold Moves for Business Growth* offers actual strategies and insight that business owners can use as an additional resource."

—**Jozelle Luster Booker**, President and CEO, The MMBC Continuum

"Carolyn Hardy, by definition, understands how to operate, lead and manage big organizations, supply chains and teams of people successfully. But what distinguishes her is the way she confronts adversity and turbulence in business which is to say, she does calmly, boldly and with an intention to grow. *Step Out* is a must read for these reasons—especially right now!"

—**Harold Ford Jr.**, Former Tennessee Congressman,
Chairman, Rx Saver,
Managing partner, HFJ Ventures

"*Step Out: Bold Moves for Business Growth* is Carolyn Hardy's newest work that finally gives us a playbook for handling the triumphs and challenges of starting and owning your own business or brand. With the fierce acumen and experience as a serial entrepreneur, Carolyn Hardy presents practical advice with head, heart, and soul.

This toolkit addresses the standard issues that many business owners face. With this book, we are no longer left to muddle through the labyrinth of entrepreneurship, but rather we are given a path to survive, thrive, and flourish.

Similar to sitting at a table with a trusted adviser over tea, *Step Out: Bold Moves for Business Growth* gives us tangible tools and unshakable faith to step out boldly and make it the business world."

—**Dr. Janet Walsh,** Owner Tea Tea and Company

"There may well be no, 'Secret to Success.' But, there is a, 'Path.' In her new book, *Step Out*, Carolyn Hardy provides a perfect primer for entrepreneurial success. In this dynamic, compelling presentation, Ms. Hardy educates, equips, enables, empowers and most significantly INSPIRES others to be entrepreneurially triumphant. Her experience and vision serve to guide one to tap into one's own wisdom, creativity, discipline and perseverance to achieve significance in business.

YOU INSPIRE ME."

—**Roby S. Williams,** President, Black Business
Association of Memphis (BBA)

"Step Out: Bold Moves for Business Growth by Carolyn Chism Hardy should be required reading for CEO's and others who want to be in the C-Suite. Ms. Hardy is a former CEO suite executive for billion-dollar companies. She now owns highly successful businesses. Carolyn knows how to lead people, launch companies that add value to society, and strengthen businesses endeavors by addressing problems business leaders face. Ms. Hardy uses her own stories to enlighten and inspire the reader, encourage beginners, and help others re-imagine their companies. I highly recommend Ms. Hardy as a person and her book for sage advice and clear direction."

—**Shirley Raines,** President Emeritus, University of
Memphis, Author, Leadership Consultant

"In a world plagued with complex problems and rapidly changing dynamics that bring traditional strategies in question, bold leadership is a necessity for the prosperity of any organization. However, bold leadership is much more than talk. *Step Out* clarifies the path forward as a leader, by rooting the work of leadership in timeless principles. Carolyn Hardy's latest book is much more than theory on transformational leadership. It is the journey map that has led to her success in business and community leadership, which she is now sharing with each of us. In any leadership opportunity, you will find this book to be helpful and handy."

—**Kenyatta Lovett,** Assistant Commissioner for Workforce Services TN Dept. of Labor and Workforce Development

"Carolyn Hardy is a visionary, leader, and entrepreneurial hero in the Memphis area, and she has served as a trusted advisor to local business owners—and to me personally. Her success and expertise are truly legendary, and her business advice is always on-point. I have no doubt that her fresh perspectives and real-life experiences in *Step Out* will inspire founders to transform their businesses or start a new venture."

—**Leslie Lynn Smith,** President and CEO Epicenter

"In *Step Out* Carolyn Hardy takes the lessons from her vast experience career as an entrepreneur and corporate executive and creates an entertaining and practical guide for business owners and corporate executives to break existing paradigms and create out of the box solutions to everyday challenges. With *Step Out* she turns her successful journey into an invaluable set of tools for you to use in navigating a complex business landscape."

—**D. Bryan Jordan,** Chairman of the Board, President and CEO First Horizon National Corporation

"*Step Out* is a true call to action for new and seasoned business owners as well as Executives that wants to transform their businesses. Carolyn's inspiring stories are motivational and her ability to simplify complex problems is uncanny. *Step Out* is one of the most useful and pragmatic books I have read in a long time. Simple, Inspirational and actionable"

—**Michael Ugwueke,** DHA, FACHE, President/CEO
Methodist Le Bonheur Health Healthcare

"Carolyn offers a compelling and important read for business owners, one full of innovative ideas, real life examples, and practical recommendations for daily operations. There's plenty to inspire business owners across the full spectrum of experience, from novice to the seasoned entrepreneur. If you're committed to doing more with less, operating in the most efficient and effective manner possible, and making sure you innovate to stay on the cutting edge, set aside time to read and study Carolyn Hardy's latest offering."

—**M. David Rudd,** Ph.D., ABPP, President,
The University of Memphis

"Carolyn is one of a few business professionals that focuses single-mindedly on multiple business processes while staying connected with multiple people in a manner that lets them know they are unique. Having access to Carolyn's thoughts in *Step Out* about how you should take bold moves for your business growth almost gives readers an unfair advantage over competitors."

—**Douglas G. Scarboro**, Senior Vice President, Memphis
Regional Executive,
The Federal Reserve Bank of St. Louis

"Carolyn once again displays how masterful she is at providing theoretical leadership guidance in a practical and personal manner. In each chapter, she challenges business owners to find the courage to *Step Out* boldly as they strategically and intentionally plan to win the growth game."

—**Dr. Tracy D. Hall,** President, Southwest Tennessee Community College

"Carolyn Hardy is one of the most notable women entrepreneurs of the 20th century. She has experienced numerous successes in her business career. One of her many crowning achievements occurred when she led an ownership group in the purchase of Coors Brewery in Memphis, which she had managed for Coors. Carolyn understands what it takes to grow a business from its infancy to a multi-million-dollar revenue business. She is a very driven and competitive businessperson, but equally personable and engaging."

—**Johnny B. Moore, Jr.**, Mid-West Tennessee Regional President, SunTrust—now Truist

"I was with Carolyn Hardy at the beginning of her journey to start her business. She faced what some would consider insurmountable obstacles including discrimination, financial, political and tornado disaster among many. Through courage, tenacity and boldness she overcame them all. Carolyn is a shining example of true American entrepreneurial spirit."

—**John W. Moore,** Former Northwest Airlines Vice President, former CEO of the Greater Memphis Chamber of Commerce and Chairman and CEO of JWMCORP

STEP OUT

BOLD
MOVES
FOR
BUSINESS
GROWTH

CAROLYN HARDY

NEW YORK

LONDON • NASHVILLE • MELBOURNE • VANCOUVER

Step Out

Bold Moves for Business Growth

Published in New York, New York, by Morgan James Publishing. Morgan James is a trademark of Morgan James, LLC. www.MorganJamesPublishing.com

ISBN 9781631951435 paperback
ISBN 9781631951442 eBook
Library of Congress Control Number: 2020936525

Cover Design by:
Rachel Lopez
www.r2cdesign.com

Interior Design by:
Chris Treccani
www.3dogcreative.net

Author Photo by:
Keoni Keur

Morgan James is a proud partner of Habitat for Humanity Peninsula and Greater Williamsburg. Partners in building since 2006.

Get involved today! Visit
MorganJamesPublishing.com/giving-back

Table of Contents

Introduction: The American Dream   xv

Chapter 1:   What it Takes   1
Chapter 2:   What's the Point?   13
Chapter 3:   The Naked Truth about Opportunities   23
Chapter 4:   Know Your Product   31
Chapter 5:   All the Time in the World? Not Really   41
Chapter 6:   Make Up Your Mind   49
Chapter 7:   Roll Out or Roll Over   61
Chapter 8:   Timing is Everything   71
Chapter 9:   The Secret Sauce to Good PR   81
Chapter 10:   The Power in People   91
Chapter 11:   Sell with Heart   99
Chapter 12:   Show Me the Money   109
Chapter 13:   Growing Pains   121
Chapter 14:   Speak Up   131
Chapter 15:   Provide Equipment   141
Chapter 16:   Signing on the Dotted Line   149
Chapter 17:   Leading the Way   159
Chapter 18:   The Right Role Models   169
Chapter 19:   Overcompensating? No Such Thing   181
Chapter 20:   Everybody Wins   189

Conclusion   197
Acknowledgments   201
Carolyn Chism Hardy Moving Mountains and Needles   205
Endnotes   209
Look Up: Five Principles of Intentional Leadership   214
The Impossible Turned Possible   217

Introduction:

The American Dream

I was the keynote speaker for the Urban League of Greater Chattanooga's annual Entrepreneur Power Luncheon two years after Shark Tank's Daymond John. Over 600 professionals and business owners—from CEOs to accountants—were in attendance. The room was charged with anticipation. My objective was to deliver an inspirational message that would motivate the audience members to achieve aspirational goals.

At the event, I met a business owner who had driven from Atlanta, Georgia to save her business. She said her business was flat and just not growing. She was seeking practical advice from someone who understood her challenges and her journey. She needed new ideas and the confidence to pursue growth. After my speech, I saw that same woman's face beaming with a glow of confidence that was missing before. She said, "You delivered. Your message provided both fresh ideas and strategies, as well as the guidance I needed for my business."

As a speaker and writer, success means touching someone's life, giving them guidance when they need it the most. But for that business owner—and for you—my guidance is only as good as the actions she takes when she returns to work with those fresh ideas and new strategies.

Who is Carolyn Chism Hardy?

Let me tell you a little about myself. I'm known for being a serial entrepreneur and trailblazer after starting my journey at an early age. I learned winning and losing playing marbles for keeps and street softball, and I learned the value of a sales pitch selling greeting cards before applying for a retail job at the corner store at twelve years old. Those lessons provided the foundation for my entrepreneurial journey. As I discuss in my first book, *Look Up: The Five Principles of Intentional Leadership*, the right character traits are critical for business success. I'm also not good at "no." When I was denied an opportunity because the company preferred candidates with a master's degree, I removed that obstacle less than two years later.

I earned a bachelor's degree in accounting and passed the CPA exam before completing my master's degree in management. For me, education has been invaluable to climbing the corporate ladder and leading my own company.

My professional career began at the J. M. Smucker Company as a staff accountant, and I was later promoted to plant controller. As plant controller, I led accounts payable, receivables, payroll, inventory control, purchasing, and financials. Later, as a quality manager, I established quality standards, monitored adherence to good manufacturing practices, quality audits, and ensured compliance with regulations. As a human resource manager, I led labor relations, safety, training, hiring, firing, complaint resolution process, progressive discipline process, insurance, and worker's compensation reporting and tracking. Developing best practices to deliver consistently was fundamental to success in each position. After my promotion to plant controller, I learned that people are the business, and the business is people. A company's performance is influenced by the skills, attitude, and commitment of the team. These roles at J.M Smucker provided a solid understanding that people, process, and purpose are connected—and the business falls apart when they are not connected.

Land of Opportunity

Small businesses, like immigrants, believe America is the "land of opportunity." Brookings Institute reports that Americans cared more about equal opportunity than about equal results,[1] and a central tenet of the American creed is the commitment to provide everyone with a fair chance to develop individual talents. This belief has deep roots in American culture and history.

And this was my dream.

I approached every business opportunity with passion, drive, and motivation in order to achieve my American dream. The American dream is our right, but equal opportunity only occurs if you demand your place in America's history.

Business owners develop products or services that benefit society. They satisfy an unmet need that is widely known, or is soon to be discovered through effective marketing. This could be a service company, supply company, a faster tool, new food or beverage, a restaurant, writing a book, selling real estate, running a blog, starting a fitness plan, or developing a software application. Instead of working for a company and being a cog in the wheel, you are the CEO. The business owner pursues their passion and runs the business the way they see fit with an equal opportunity for success as the other business owners also chasing their passions and running their businesses to benefit society.

John Maxwell, famous writer and author, once wrote, "Successful and unsuccessful people do not vary greatly in their abilities. They vary in their desires to reach their potential." This desire to reach your potential, to seize your equal opportunity, requires using every resource at your disposal to achieve success.

Family Business

My family has a history of business ownership. My uncle worked in construction, and the quality of his family's life was much better than my family's life—or that of anyone I knew. He purchased a new home; his children wore new clothes and ate three meals a day. His children also went on to start a chain of grocery stores that grew to an amazing scale over twenty-five years before closing in early 2000.

On the other hand, I lived in poverty during my first twelve years of life. We were lucky to get one meal a day, which sometimes was a fried onion. New clothes were secondhand, but they were new to me. My father, Sidney Chism, worked two jobs to provide food, clothing, and shelter for a family of sixteen. He was a delivery driver by day and a plumber by night. Dad's employer, Gordon Hollingsworth, closed in the late 1970s and his side hustle became his full-time business. He soon learned that business ownership doubled, sometimes even tripled, his annual earning.

When I made the switch to business ownership, I went from being an employee at a billion-dollar brewing company to owning the facility and starting Hardy Bottling. My education and experience working for other companies were invaluable for researching and writing my first business plan. My professional career provided a broad range of experiences, including working with lawyers, negotiating contracts, procurement, insurance, marketing, building relationships, and much more. Although I had plenty of good examples in my family, my success opening my first company would not have been possible without this professional exposure. But when the brewing company announced it was closing the facility, it was time to start my journey toward achieving my American dream.

How Can I Help More?

When I spoke at the Urban League's luncheon, I was happy to be that business owner's inspiration and to provide some guidance for her through my presentation.

But I had to ask: How can I help people everywhere take advantage of my experience when they need it the most? I want to help *you* save your business. I want to help business owners grow on a larger scale than one luncheon speech at a time. I want to share creative ideas that spur creative solutions to complex business problems.

I know that you as a business owner give everything and more to succeed. Take comfort in knowing you are not the first, nor will you be the last, to face challenges. In *Step Out*, I will teach you how to analyze opportunities, identify and mitigate risks, understand and plan for the financial impact by developing action plans, and so much more. *Step Out* is that companion that can speak to you when you need it the most.

Step Out shares my life experiences, both good and bad. I share stories about business challenges and lay out common sense solutions that fit most businesses. The stories of my best practices cover a broad range of topics from legal and licensing to financial management, working capital for expansion to sales and marketing, insurance, human resources, and other aspects of business. Each chapter communicates a bold move you can take to grow—or save—your business. Perhaps most important are the suggested actions found at the end of each chapter. For what good is my guidance unless you put it to use?

The American dream is alive and well. The challenge lies in that the world is complicated. Change is occurring in milliseconds versus decades, the competition is global, and access to capital remains limited to the few. *Step Out* eases your burden on this business ownership journey by arming you with creative ideas to complex problems. I hope this book becomes your friend and the best-kept secret in your arsenal for avoiding costly mistakes. Adding *Step Out* to your tool kit gives you the edge with real-time practical next steps and motivation.

Let's get started on your journey to achieving your American dream.

Chapter 1:

What it Takes

During my career, I managed several large manufacturing plants and improved each one's performance. After arriving to do the same at Coors Brewing Company, I recognized the plant was in trouble. The facility had the highest costs and the poorest safety record, along with many quality challenges. Local leadership's reputation was extremely poor with corporate leadership. To make matters worse, employees on all levels believed that Coors would never close this facility since they recently had invested 100 million dollars to upgrade it. No one seemed to understand that the investment was a sunk cost. Companies in Corporate America have a fiduciary responsibility to shareholders to optimize returns, which included this plant closure for Coors. My years at Coors taught me to strive for the impossible, which is the plight of most entrepreneurs.

The major disappointment finally came when Coors made the decision to close the plant due to low market share in the South. When I came to manage the facility, my boss never set an expectation for me to move the plant to a better market! Planning my next career move after Coors made its decision,

I interviewed with several large beverage manufacturers. When my contract with Coors expired, I planned to pursue opportunities with another large beverage brand. My career path had several viable alternatives to ensure I landed a great opportunity.

My practical mind said I should play it safe, keep the cushy VP job, but my heart said maybe it was time to pursue my dream of business ownership. In the end, I decided the cushy VP job required me to follow someone else's dreams. And it was time for me to follow my dream.

When the time came to close the plant, Coors officially advertised it was selling the facility for 40 million dollars. That price almost squashed my dreams—it was more than I could borrow. But I continued quietly working on my business plan for contract beverage manufacturing. The knowledge I gained developing that plan increased my confidence to pursue the purchase, and, after the brewery had been on the market for over six months, the pool of qualified buyers was down to one prospect.

During a meeting with the VP of finance at Coors, I asked about that one buyer's bid versus what the company would accept. He told me Coors's new asking price range was *one-third of the published price*! So, when the chamber of commerce asked about the status of the facility sale, I told them, "There is currently one bidder, but I would like to purchase the facility."

I spent eight months on that deal. It was exciting, frustrating, annoying, intimidating, and eye-opening. I will say, the worst realization was seeing those who should have supported me choose not to; however, those who did support me fortified my resolve to complete that deal. That deal felt like one of those smackdowns you see on wrestling commercials. My smackdown was rejection, disappointment, and intimidation, but I was ready.

Without strong character traits, I do not believe success would have been my outcome on this deal. My resilience, tenacity, integrity, relationships, and network helped me navigate this complex business transaction. Entrepreneurs and leaders are required to find real-time solutions to unexpected problems. During the process of closing that deal, I faced rejection but continued to find creative solutions, and I grew professionally. An entrepreneur faces complexities that are emotionally challenging but must continue the journey by creating new approaches and strategies—again and again!

Tenacity

Tenacity is a quality displayed by someone who just won't quit, someone who just keeps trying until they reach their goal. During the process of closing the deal on that facility, I was required to present Coors with a letter from a financial institution confirming that institution would provide the loan for me to purchase the facility and assets. That letter was due by a set date. The timeline caused me to seek many financial options simultaneously as well as pitch to potential equity investors.

I pitched to every major bank in Memphis. One memorable presentation was so comforting that the commercial banker went to sleep while his subordinate listened attentively. I continued to pitch, but it hurt. Either I was a bore, or he had already made up his mind to say no and was using the time to re-energize for the balance of his day. Despite the commercial banker missing the presentation, this bank led me to believe the loan was possible. The term sheet would take several weeks while they evaluated my application. After two weeks, I called for an update. A week later, I called again. This process continued for months.

Finally, I called the commercial banker and told him he needed to have the decency to say "no" rather than lead me on. I told him leading me on and wasting my time was a threat to the deal. He needed to have the guts to say "no" as soon as possible. If I had not insisted upon closure, this runaround could have caused me to miss the contractual deadline for the letter. I had to exercise tenacity to take control of this situation since time was not on my side. Coors wanted me to miss the date to terminate the deal. I was not going to let that happen. Entrepreneurs must know when to take control to bring closure when others will not. Time is your most precious commodity. I was taught early in my career to give others a graceful way out but to get out as soon as possible when there's not going to be a deal.

Another bank gave me a term sheet a few weeks after my application and presentation. I was feeling good and thought they might be the one. Wrong—the deal was not intended to close. The term sheet was a carrot and the rules kept changing. The first term sheet required me to sign with partners I did not respect and negotiate a contract with the Teamsters Union. The second term sheet stated I needed a guarantor for three million dollars of the loan. After I met that requirement, they changed the guarantor's terms again. It seemed like the bank was trying to find a number or condition I could not meet. This bank went past ridiculous to the point of insulting.

What's worse: one commercial banker sleeping then leading me on or the other thinking I was a fool? The one thing they had in common: They both hurt me. But their disrespect and superior attitudes only increased my drive and determination to seek other options for financing. At no point was failure an option.

Resilience

Resilience is the ability to bounce back after major disappointments, which, in business, will be numerous and often, without being overwhelmed or acting in dysfunctional or harmful ways. Business owners get a lot of rejections whether from deals, bank financing, or any number of other reasons. As a rule, small businesses get "no" more frequently than "yes."

In pursuit of that same deal, I pitched to many businessmen, including a local dentist. It was late and raining, and the meeting was in his office. The deer-in-the-headlight look told me everything I needed to know. This deal was either over his head and/or over his bank account. I needed to let him down gracefully and move on. When I was driving away, the voice in the back of my head asked, "What are you doing?" I was tired, overworked, and frustrated. But as usual, the next morning I was fresh, feeling resilient and ready to take on the world again. Next banker or potential investor, here I come.

During this time, I met a former employee of Merrill Lynch. He told me that a bank would not loan a first-time business owner the fifteen to twenty-five million dollars I was asking for. He said they would waste my time, and this had been my experience. Banks do not have the appetite for the risk of that size loan with a new business owner. That contact then introduced me to a hard moneylender from Oklahoma who represented me in my quest to secure a loan. I updated my business plan with all my learning from the many rejections. Within two weeks after my pitch to new lenders, I received a term sheet. Sixty days later, the purchase contract was complete within the set timeline. Securing a loan may have looked hopeless at times, but resilience and determination took me over the finish line.

Successful businesses do not accept "no" without an explanation. When a prospect tells me no, I always ask "Why?" Asking "Why" (Y) allows me to understand the problem and accurately address it. If I understand Y, I can solve for X (the result I am seeking). If you do not know Y, it limits your ability to address the real reason for the "no." It's impossible to solve an unknown problem. Remember, always ask why—a closed mouth does not get fed.

Integrity

Integrity is tested when the chips are down. That is also when integrity is needed the most. Integrity is the practice of being honest and showing a consistent and uncompromising adherence to strong moral and ethical principles and values. Integrity is regarded as the honesty and truthfulness or accuracy of one's actions.

I had potential investors who wanted to partner with me on the deal. They proposed that I would control the business on paper, while they legally controlled the company. I told them I planned to be the majority owner since it was my deal, and I was willing to invest 51 percent of the capital to maintain control. The investors said I could not afford this deal; therefore, I needed them. I had spent most of my career playing second fiddle. I was starting my own company to be my own boss. As I interviewed potential partners, this conversation was the norm. If anyone was to become my partner, they wanted to be the majority owner. It became obvious that this was my journey alone. It was time for me to write my narrative and follow it, so I said goodbye to investors. Frankly, most of the prospective investors were not familiar or comfortable with a black female as the majority owner. I could accept that, knowing the journey wouldn't end after securing financing; therefore, I proceeded without a partner and did it my way. I felt like it was either now or never.

Relationships and Networking

Wikipedia defines networking as a socioeconomic business activity by which businesspeople and entrepreneurs meet to form business relationships and to recognize, create, or act upon business opportunities, share information, and seek potential partners for ventures.[2] Networking does not mean that your church friend or relative knows someone's name. An ideal networking relationship is an individual who can connect you with key decision-makers or those with the authority to influence decisions.

Beyond the basic definition of networking, entrepreneurs must know a little about everything, and they must find ways to gain access to that experience and knowledge they need to start and grow their business. Enter networking. If you don't have prior experience, the services and knowledge needed to start your business can be gained from many nonprofit groups in your community. For example, most chambers of commerce provide small business with information, training, resources, and contacts for local, state, and federal agencies. The chamber's members also offer a wide range of services and can attest to the integrity of the membership.

Another resource could be entrepreneur incubators, which are community-based organizations that help entrepreneurs who are in the early stage of their business or looking to grow their business. An example of an incubator is Epicenter. The website reads: "Epicenter exists to connect, support and expand the entrepreneurial ecosystem in the Memphis area. We aim to serve entrepreneurs, creators and organizations who are committed to helping businesses strive in our community."[3] They offer training, guidance, some funding, and contacts for entrepreneurs looking to start or grow a business. In addition, they provide contacts for banking relationships, website development, business development, marketing, etc. They also sponsor programs for matchmaking such as pitch night where entrepreneurs pitch to angel investors or venture capitalists.[4]

In addition, local universities typically have access to volunteer retired business professionals who are willing to mentor small businesses and entrepreneurs. These retired business professionals usually come from a broad range of professions.

Typically, services similar to the chamber of commerce, Epicenter, and local universities to support small business are free, but it does require the business owner put pride aside and be open to advice from others. Remember, no one expects you to know everything but you.

What does it take?

Business owners must thrive in complex situations, be objective, and work in ambiguity. The business owner and their team collectively must understand all aspects of the business. When an opportunity is presented, they should be able to immediately access their capabilities to protect their customers. The entrepreneur's role is to be an expert in their offering.

For example, when a customer's recipe required us to produce a highly carbonated beverage and pasteurize it at high temperatures, we knew and advised the customer that specification would not work with our system. We recommended lowering the pasteurization temperature. Otherwise, the cans would explode, destroying the customer's product. We ran a limited test to demonstrate the problem. The customer was appreciative of my team's knowledge and followed our recommendation. Customers expect you, your team, and your network to be the expert in your offering, so use your resources and act like it. Do not rely on excuses and make sure your customers or prospects have no reason to lose confidence in your business.

Unlike a job, business owners own all the problems of the business. A business owner is responsible for everything, which means the buck starts and stops with you. Be prepared to work hard and long hours as you birth your dream. Place your sanity on the shelf for a few years. Business ownership is an emotional roller coaster, but the positive energy from your good days will help you survive the bad ones. And, trust me, you will have both.

So, what does it take to be an entrepreneur or small business owner? Everything you have and more.

Based upon your reading about "What it Takes," what actions will you take? Suggestions:

Do you have a business plan or business strategy? Creating a business plan will focus you and your team on a common path. It can also flesh out opportunities to ensure they are realistically feasible.

_____

_____

_____

Create a list of skills and experience gaps to use as part of your selection criteria for your next hire or consultant.

_____

_____

_____

Join one board or volunteer organization in the next year that advances your skills and grows your business network.

_____

_____

_____

Chapter 2:

What's the Point?

The J. M. Smucker Company purchased the Mrs. Smith's Pie brand from Kellogg because the brand complimented Smucker's existing product lines. Smucker's was the leader in the jam and jelly industry. They were experienced at procuring fruit from both U.S. and international markets. Quality was integrated into everything they did, including their well-known slogan: "With a name like Smucker's, it has to be good." Smucker's understood the grocery retail market and had experience working with labor unions.

With those strengths and obvious synergies, what caused Smucker's pie business to ultimately fail? Well, the unanticipated problems from the frozen pie supply chain were foreign to Smucker's. Smucker's executives did not understand the complexity of frozen products supply chain management. The jelly products they were familiar with are transported and warehoused at ambient or room temperature throughout the distribution network. Frozen pies, on the other hand, must be transported and warehoused at temperatures that ensure products remain frozen. The frozen supply chain was the exact opposite of Smucker's expertise, and their lack of experience caused Smucker's to sell Mrs. Smith's Pie brand for less than one-third of the ninety million dollars they originally paid for it.

What you don't know will hurt you, and, typically, the pain is felt on the bottom line.

So, why grow?

With all the risk, what's the point of growing your business? There are a few companies out there that purposely stay small, companies the industry calls a "lifestyle company." A lifestyle company's only goal is to earn enough profits to support the owner's lifestyle. But most business owners dream bigger. They want more for their business. The point of growing is to take advantage of opportunities created by new demand. The point is to use your strengths to expand and grow. The point is to scale up to reduce per unit overhead cost. The point is to become a market leader. The point is to grow your business, to know where you are going and why. A word of warning from Smucker's story: It's also important to know what you don't know. If you recognize what you don't know and grow right, you can minimize your risk of business failure during growth.

Understanding Opportunities

The first step to revealing if a business opportunity for growth is worth pursuing is research. It is critical to reduce your options for growth and focus on the ideas with the highest probability of success. The danger of pursuing too many growth opportunities can be just as risky as doing nothing.

Your research should include information about the size of the market. I always tell business owners and salesmen that the best customer they have is the customer they have. Small businesses should pursue business expansion in their current service offering. For example, an electrical supplier could expand by offering other building products, such as lighting, cables, filters, etc. These expansions typically are low-risk and low-cost. They tend to leverage current infrastructure and human capital. The key to this strategy is to first target your existing customers before expanding to new customers. Your existing customers are already familiar with your great service, and they desire one-stop shopping.

Once you have expanded in your current service offering, the next step can be to expand your offering outside of your current geography and industry.

Your research should also explore how the opportunity for growth could be impacted by the business environment, such as government regulations, economic indicators, and trade policies. Understanding the business environment is critical for accessing the risks and rewards associated with the opportunity.

Transloading Research and Evaluation

After I sold Hardy Bottling, my first business, I evaluated ideas for my next business venture. My knowledge of supply chain management, the logistics industry, and the excess supply of empty containers in Memphis led me to consider transloading; thus, Henderson Transloading came about.

Retail transloading is a "hub and spoke" model similar to passenger airlines. The products, like passengers with a connecting flight, are taken to a central hub. Truckloads of goods are shipped to a warehouse from many brand manufacturers. Sending large volumes of a SKU to a hub and only reshipping a limited quantity for a planned time supply reduced inventory cost, transportation cost, and the space needed to warehouse goods.

Grain or bulk transloaders transfer goods from one mode of transportation to another. For example, my company transfers grain received in hopper trucks into containers. Products are typically transloaded to reduce transportation costs and/or to improve handling costs at the destination. The transloader at various transfer points moves goods into a cheaper or more efficient transportation mode. Typically, a hopper truck of grain driven from Arkansas to California would cost over 5,000 dollars while shipping a container on a railcar holding 20 percent more grain reduces the freight cost to under 1,500 dollars.

In order to evaluate the feasibility of transloading in the Memphis area, I sourced information from the University of Memphis, the USDA, and the regional chamber of commerce. This research was critical for analyzing the types of transloading, the market, barriers to entry, and key differentiators to succeed in this market. The data that became critical to my decision was as follows:

- The USDA OSCAR reports empty container availability in the United States by location, including each port. The Memphis supply of empty containers was created by imports from China into the Memphis market. Memphis's inland port had the highest number of empty containers compared to other U.S. inland ports due to limited exports from Memphis.

- Memphis, Chicago, and Kansas are the only cities in the U.S. with five Class 1 railroads.

- Based upon our central location, 70 percent of U.S. destinations can be reached in less than one day from Memphis.

- Memphis is surrounded by thirteen million acres of six major crops from Arkansas, Tennessee, and Mississippi.

- Tariffs and trade laws associated with political and social changes influenced the business environment for international trade. The research showed that mitigating the risks associated with the business environment required diversification of grain handling.

Additionally, Henderson Transloading interviewed major companies with transloading export and distribution expertise to understand the types of transloading services most needed and the expectations for those services. We used this information to perform an industry analysis to assess the competitive dynamics of the transloading industry. Henderson would be the only grain transloader in the market, plus the market already had all the other services it needed to be successful. The fatal flaw was that this market had very few direct customers and an uncontrollable business environment that involved tariffs, China, and U.S. trade disputes. Also, the larger customers were in Chicago and Kansas. The major external factors impacting grain transloading were the government, weather, export demand, grain costs, and tariffs.

We would not have understood these risks without doing our research. The industry analysis also identified other types of transloaders in the region, and this assessment identified both the opportunity to handle grain and the potential threats we might face. The key to surviving our ever-changing business environment is to understand the differences between your business and those of your competitors and how to use that knowledge to your advantage both in the present and in the future.

During the research process, be bold about reaching out to get vital information from industry leaders. The worst response you can get from the leader is "no." During the research stage, the cost of the venture is mostly your time. Then, with knowledge in hand, analyze whether you are ready.

Opportunity Knocks

Our research revealed that Memphis was an ideal location for grain and bulk transloading for the reasons outlined above, despite the risks, but we estimated that we would need a year to implement the plan. After reviewing the service offering of competitors, we offered services we could consistently deliver at competitive prices. We controlled most services required for transloading and did not offer services with fluctuating prices because customers required fixed contract prices effective for six to twelve months at a time.

Less than a month after our research and evaluation, a grain merchandiser contacted us to transload his grain. The prospect stated he needed a transloader for dried distiller's grain. I asked when the services would be required. He needed transloading services in one month. I told him I would be ready in twelve months. The prospect countered by offering to supply all equipment if Henderson would supply the site and labor. I answered, "Yes, but let's negotiate a contract to ensure we both understand the rules of engagement." A contract minimizes the risk of any misunderstanding relative to the scope of services, pricing, responsibilities, the parties, payment terms, etc. (more on this later). This was my opportunity to start a new business with minimal capital investment, which further reduced the risk of pursing this opportunity.

And we seized that opportunity.

So, what's the point?

So, what's the point of seizing a business opportunity? Do you know what you don't know or how you will fill the gaps? Do you understand the pros and cons of your new offerings as they relate to your current business? Business research should narrow your focus on what to pursue and identify competitors and risks associated with the opportunity. The point is to listen to the data rather than manipulate the data to fit your desired outcome.

Remember that all business is not good business. Your research might reveal that the business idea does not have a clear value proposition compared to the competition. Business does not earn a profit when cost is greater than the sales price or margins are slim. If margins are too slim, you cannot afford a mistake or absorb minor cost increases, which could result in bankruptcy. Pass on those opportunities.

Colin Powell, an American politician, retired four-star general in the United States Army, and US national security advisor, said, "There are no secrets to success. It is the result of preparation, hard work and learning from failure." Effectively researching business ideas is the preparation required to evaluate those ideas, while hard work will be required to execute them. Your willingness to learn from failure and make timely course corrections during the implementation of a new opportunity will impact the long-term success of any new business venture. A new business idea executed well will deliver the growth your business and you deserve.

Based upon your reading about "What's the Point?," what actions will you take? Suggestions:

As you think through your business, write down creative ways to grow your business.

_____

_____

_____

Think of your top three competitors. What other services do they offer? What's stopping you from expanding? What competitive advantage can you offer?

_____

_____

_____

What services are you outsourcing that you could perform with a minimum investment for existing customers? Remember, you have the most credibility with your current customers.

_____

_____

_____

Chapter 3:

The Naked Truth about Opportunities

Why Use SWOT

Socrates, a classical philosopher, wrote, "I know you won't believe me, but the highest form of Human Excellence is to question oneself and others." The investment to start Henderson Transloading was several million dollars for equipment, the facility, and site improvements. This investment was only made after a thorough SWOT analysis, a one-year successful pilot, and meetings with large, successful transloaders to validate our decision.

Socrates's advice is still valid over a thousand years later. Today, SWOT is a systematic method to question yourself and others. SWOT is an acronym that stands for Strengths, Weaknesses, Opportunities, and Threats. A SWOT analysis is a list of your business's strengths, weaknesses, opportunities, and threats. It's a great tool for businesses to use to systematically assess and understand a changing environment, business expansion, or new business opportunity.[5]

Strengths and weaknesses are internal things, such as reputation, patents, capabilities, capacity, staffing, skills, location, and services. You can work to change weaknesses over time, but not without some work and/or investment. Opportunities and threats are external things, such as technology, suppliers, competitors, and prices controlled by market forces. They happen whether you like it or not. You can't change them.

SWOT allows you to respond proactively to identified threats, weaknesses, and opportunities. I recommend conducting a strategy meeting at least once a year that begins with a SWOT analysis. (If Smucker's had used SWOT, they might have identified the threat associated with handling frozen products and developed a strategy to minimize risk of failure.)

New businesses should also use SWOT as a part of their planning process. There is never a one-size-fits-all plan for business and thinking about your new business in terms of its unique SWOT will put you on the right track, right away, and save you from a lot of headaches while minimizing business losses down the road.

Henderson Truths

With Henderson Transloading, I performed a SWOT analysis on the different types of transloading. The SWOT included an analysis of strengths and weaknesses. The following are questions we asked to analyze the attributes of transloading within our control:

- Where does the business excel?
- Where does the business fall short?

- What are the positive and negative attributes of people, such as their knowledge, background, education, credentials, network, reputation, or skills?
- What are the tangible assets of the company, such as capital, credit, existing customers or distribution channels, patents, or technologies?
- What advantages or disadvantages do we have over the competition?
- What other values offer a competitive advantage or disadvantage?
- What areas need improvement to accomplish the business objectives or compete with the strongest competitor?

Henderson's inherent strengths were container availability, five Class 1 railroads, proximity to a major growing region, co-location with the BNSF railroad, customized software integrated with the transloading system, proximity to competitors, supply chain knowledge, etc. Henderson's weaknesses were the lack of grain merchandising skills, the lack of an in-house trucking company, no long-term contracts, and low availability of a skilled workforce.

External Truths

The next section of the SWOT analyzes threats and opportunities. Opportunities are external factors that represent reasons your business is likely to prosper. Threats include external factors beyond your control that could place your strategy, or the business, at risk. You have no control over these situations, but you may benefit from having contingency plans to address threats if they should occur. The questions we asked were:

- What opportunities exist in the market or the environment that the business can benefit from?
- Is the industry perception of the business positive?
- Has there been recent market growth or other changes in the market to create opportunities?
- Is the opportunity ongoing, or is there only a limited window for it?
- Who are the potential competitors?
- What factors beyond the business's control could place it at risk?
- Has there been a significant change in supplier prices or the availability of raw materials?
- What about shifts in consumer behavior, the economy, or government regulations that could reduce sales?
- Has a new product or technology been introduced that makes the business's products, equipment, or services obsolete?

Retail transloading for consumer packaged goods requires a facility with hundreds of forklifts and hundreds of employees. This costs millions of dollars in capital and working capital to create a complex operation. Grain transloading, on the other hand, required a tractor, auger, and scale with no facility. At startup, we outsourced the labor and management. The cost of a basic operation was less than 150,000 dollars, as opposed to millions of dollars. The higher the initial investment is, the greater the risk. The grain transloading risk initially was the lowest.

The SWOT on Henderson initially revealed the most significant threat as our inability to compete with barges, as well as unstable commodity prices. For example, the president's tariff on China caused grain sales to drop over 30 percent. The next year, China accused the U.S. of anti-dumping, which bankrupted many merchandisers. This change in government regulations was beyond my control but still placed our business at risk.

Great businesses know when an opportunity is worth pursuing. My experience and knowledge of logistics indicated that grain transloading was a good opportunity. The research provided data supporting our pursuit of the opportunity, and we did a thorough SWOT analysis to understand potential threats and current weaknesses.

The Elephant in the Room

Business owners have two ways to learn about their weaknesses and threats: either by using SWOT or watching the process fail and impact customer service and costs. The business world is complex, but a SWOT analysis will identify the internal and external forces that may impact your business positively or negatively. The challenge most businesses face is looking at the world through rose-colored glasses. Most businesses see what they want to see, not the business as it really is. A thorough analysis can help overcome that tendency.

> *Stop focusing on ants while your business is being run over by elephants.*

Currently, Henderson's elephant is the president's tariff, and we may not have recognized that elephant without our regular analysis. Take the time to understand your business or new opportunity in a systematic way by using SWOT. Socrates realized the need to understand the naked truth about opportunities. And the truth is, waiting to respond to unexpected or unseen threats that ultimately lead to failures is not a strategy used by successful business owners. Have the sense to take off the rose-colored glasses, examine your business, and see the truth.

Based upon your reading about "The Naked Truth about Opportunities," What actions will you take? Suggestions:

What opportunities exist in your market or the environment that you can benefit from? Has there been recent market growth or have there been other changes in the market to create an opportunity?

_____

_____

_____

What factors beyond your control (threats) could place your business at risk? Has there been a significant change in supplier prices or the availability of raw materials, shifts in consumer behavior, the economy, or government regulations that could reduce your sales? Has a new product or technology been introduced that makes your products, equipment, or services obsolete?

_____

_____

_____

List your strengths and weaknesses. Ask yourself: What do you do well or poorly? What are the positive and negative attributes of people, such as their knowledge, background, education, credentials, network, reputation, or skills? What are the tangible assets of the company, such as capital, credit, existing customers or distribution channels, patents, or technologies? What advantages or disadvantages do you have over your competition? What other positive or negative aspects, internal to your business, add value or offer you a competitive advantage or disadvantage? What areas need improvement to accomplish your objectives?

Strengths:

_____

_____

_____

Weaknesses:

_____

_____

_____

Chapter 4:

Know Your Product

Has your competence ever been tested at the most inconvenient times? Sadly, bad news does not wear a watch. It does not know when you are asleep or that now is not a good time.

One time, during a tour of the manufacturing plant that was producing jams and jellies, Tim Smucker, CEO of the J. M. Smucker Company, tested whether I knew the quality of the products that were being made. At the time, I was quality manager—my team was responsible for monitoring product quality—and Tim's management style was management by walking around so he could hear about the operations performance directly from employees. During a previous visit to the lab, he asked the USDA inspector about the quality of the strawberry preserves being produced. And the USDA inspector said, "The strawberry preserves have no whole strawberries!"

Since I was the quality manager, Tim asked me about the USDA inspector's concern. I was taken aback momentarily, but I calmly said to Tim, "Let's go for a walk." I wanted him to judge the product himself at the inspection table where all whole fruit products flowed prior to filling. The inspection table and the jars of finished product were filled with strawberries. I knew the quality of our strawberry preserves was top-notch with lots of strawberries. But allowing Tim to observe real-time production without hesitation demonstrated my confidence that the quality of the product was not an issue. The USDA inspector later stated that he was nervous and blurted out what he said. Why couldn't his nervousness cause him to say something positive? Thankfully my team and I knew our product. Knowing your product requires team members who are responsible for execution to know the product's manufacturing processes and quality expectations as well.

Brand Ambassadors

Years later, we developed a course entitled *Jelly Making 101* at Smucker's. The course was designed to teach employees our quality standards. We taught the basic process to all employees: fruit sourcing, vacuum processing, product profiles, essence recovery, and packaging. Our objective was for each employee to own the quality of the product and to become the frontline of quality control as well as our best brand ambassador. Employees were already proud of Smucker's products, but now they could articulate with great confidence specific details that created the products' unique properties. After being provided the basic training, employees wanted to learn more about both the products and the company.

Employee knowledge yielded immediate payoff in ideation sessions. For example, we needed to resolve a safety risk when handling drums of white grape juice. An employee recommended installing an unloading system at the receiving dock by connecting to an existing delivery system. That employee's knowledge of the process was critical in developing the idea to connect the piping and a pump that cost 50,000 dollars to 500,000 dollars of underutilized equipment. This eliminated unsafe drum handling, reduced manpower, and increased efficiency. The system was later implemented at two other plants, improving safety and saving millions of dollars. Employees' product knowledge and Smucker's encouragement of out-of-the-box thinking laid the foundation for improving quality and efficiency. Our willingness to train, transparency about our products, and employee inclusion in process improvements created a sense of pride, which is priceless. Not only did this solve the immediate safety risk, but also trust was improved between management and employees through increased engagement and communication.

Training Produces Real-time Experts

Employee skills and knowledge are crucial for addressing the challenges organizations face today. Problems are best addressed as they occur rather than waiting for permission from a single expert. My team at Smucker's used several methods to boost product knowledge, such as *Jelly Making 101*. We used simple terms understood by all employees with easily relatable examples. Grape jelly was our simplest product; therefore, it was used as our teaching model. Its simple ingredients and production process were easy to teach and easy for employees to remember. The product is made from corn syrup, grape juice, water, pectin, and acids. The grape jelly workflow was integrated into every new product training session. When we trained employees on one of our complex products, we simply explained that the process was the exact opposite of grape jelly. We asked employees to add the ingredients in reverse order from the familiar example, which was easy to remember since they knew the grape jelly process so well. Each employee was able to correctly manage the workflow for this complex product because they were comfortable with the basic grape jelly process. We soon became efficient at applying other variations to grape jelly workflow. This training was so effective that Smucker's added *Jelly Making 101* to our onboarding process for all new hires.

Employee training proved more effective when they were allowed to touch, taste, and feel the product. This approach teaches them how to relate to the product from the perspective of the consumer. We allowed employees to taste grape jelly with and without essence. It was obvious after tasting the different products why essence was key to quality. No training book is going to be able to authentically and completely translate product knowledge. It is merely a cookbook. In order to produce consistent product quality, employees needed access to the product experience. We later required every employee to participate in product tastings to evaluate the quality of each week's production. They provided the customer's perspectives about the product. Their opinions mattered since they had the ability to provide immediate feedback, and they had to eat their own production. Employee involvement through input in the production process creates a sense of connection and pride for the employee in the product. These intangible benefits are crucial for employee engagement and effective branding.

Product Knowledge Leads to New Ideas

Employee product knowledge and engagement also gave employees the confidence to share new ideas. For example, we were struggling to find a faster method to remove cherry pits from our system. The original method required two hours to flush the entire system with water. We would fill vessels for thirty minutes, flush, and repeat that several times. One day, an employee shared his idea of filling unused vessels in advance and flushing as soon as the line went down. This would reduce the time required from two hours to forty-five minutes. Our willingness to listen opened the lines of communications between employee and management, and employees began to make a game of recommending new ideas. Each employee wanted to find solutions to complex problems. This gave them recognition and personal pride. We awarded our roving leaders with a leader of the month plaque and jacket. Everyone wanted to win and earn their badge of honor. But this game only worked because management was open-minded, objective, and worked hand-in-hand with employees to implement change.

Companies often test new processes before implementation. This includes new technology, new equipment, or new products. And the best people to perform these tests are those who will be using or interacting with them every day. This serves to train employees at the same time as showing confidence in the team. There was a bank I was consulting with, and I was speaking with bank executives about inclusiveness. I mentioned a new bank layout at one of their branches and asked if employees understood the objective of the new layout. Were tellers allowed to review the plans and to provide input prior to implementation? I did not get a response to this question. No response speaks volumes. I was confidant employees were not consulted. The company missed an opportunity to identify their roving leaders, gain buy-in for the change, and demonstrate confidence in their employees to build long-term loyalty and brand ambassadors.

In another example, after my daughters, Jennifer, Whitney and I planned to build a new grain transloading facility. In addition to the employees, we reviewed our plans with the truck drivers who would be delivering grain to our facility. This system was key to efficient delivery of the grain. Truck drivers want to deliver to efficient facilities that allow them to make several trips per day so they can improve their bottom line. We received grain originally destined for other companies because we were efficient and our facility provided coverage in bad weather. We understood our process, but these drivers were the experts in their process. By being inclusive of their expertise and opinion, our business was able to integrate the products and services that went into the grain workflow, giving us a competitive advantage. The payoff was more business.

The Pro

At Industrial Sales, I attended sales calls with my external sales manager. During each meeting, he demonstrated he understood our products and customer needs. The internal general manager meets with contractors at counter sales to discuss projects. Collectively, the two communicate to customers that we are 'The Pro.' The difference between great and mediocre salespeople is an intimate understanding of the customer and the product offering. Improving employee knowledge builds self-esteem while adding value to customer service, resulting in increased customer confidence in your business. Knowing your products and services improves brand loyalty, consumer relationships, employee confidence and pride, product quality, and ease of selling, which, again, directly translates to your bottom line.

If you recognize a need to increase your own knowledge, entrepreneurs and small business owners have access to training from many sources. Local trade groups often provide training in their area of expertise, certification agencies and entrepreneur agencies provide general business training, and chambers of commerce and nonprofit groups have inexpensive lunch-and-learn sessions. The events are typically scheduled to respect the small business schedule by hosting breakfast or after-hours events. In addition to training, small businesses can expand their network with people who work in IT, marketing, sales, and many other professions who may provide services they need for business growth.

When I became quality manager, the quality manager at Smucker's largest plant trained me and became my mentor. Prior to starting that training, I read every manual, formula, consumer complaint, and audit having to do with the operations. I wanted to learn everything about our products. Today, in addition to seminars, training on most topics is delivered through online channels like webinars. There are industry white papers, blogs, shared files, social media, etc., with professionals in your industry willing to answer questions or participate in a healthy intellectual exchange. Access to training is at your fingertips.

To summarize, it was stated best by writer and poet Hortense Canady: "If you don't realize there is always somebody who knows how to do something better than you, then you don't give proper respects for others' talents." I learned that if you want consumers to be loyal, you must start with employee loyalty. Training employees about your product and processes creates that loyalty. You only win if your team members are not only competent in their roles but also confident. In small businesses, every employee is valuable since each one carries their share of the workload. Few small businesses have redundant staffing. Therefore, small business training is paramount to your ability to scale up your business since their knowledge contributes directly to the business's reputation. Brand ambassadors are not born but are the product of great training. Growing companies understand that the best quality manager and expert is an employee who knows your product.

Based upon your reading about "Know Your Product," what actions will you take? Suggestions:

Meet with your team to discuss your products and services. Ask them about their knowledge of your products and services. What else do they need to know? Can you produce your own 101 training class?

_____

_____

_____

Make a list of online training classes available for your products or services. For example, an air conditioning company representing a brand can get online service training courses from that brand. If you sell makeup, that brand typically has YouTube videos about best practices.

Make a list of product experts inside and outside your business. How can you learn from them and share their knowledge with your team? Try your own lunch-and-learn session for your small business, even if that means playing a short video.

Chapter 5:

All the Time in the World? Not Really

Ten months after Coors announced its plans to close the Memphis operation, the facility and equipment were officially advertised for sale. After the announcement, other companies approached me with job opportunities, and I interviewed with several major beverage companies. But I was also writing a business plan outlining my hopes and dreams of starting a contract beverage operation. Coors's original asking price of forty million dollars caused me to keep those plans a secret.

I knew that most people at Coors and in Memphis did not believe I could pull off the purchase of the brewery facility. In January, I met the only remaining prospect to purchase the brewery: City Brewing Company. City Brewery was owned by a group of successful executives. The partnership was very impressive.

The week of Dr. King's holiday, my confidence to pursue the purchase grew. As I described in an earlier chapter, I was attending a board meeting when the chamber of commerce inquired about the status of the brewery sale. I told him all prospects had declined except one bidder. More importantly, I told them I would like to make the purchase. On Friday of that same week, Coors asked me to consider a transfer to Shenandoah, Virginia to manage the startup of its new brewery, which cost 300 million dollars. They asked me to think about what job within Coors would make me happy professionally, and they wanted a response by Monday. Later that day, I asked the VP of finance at Coors about the buyer's potential bid for the facility and what Coors would accept. He told me Coors's new price was one-third the published price!

So, on Monday morning, I met with the Coors COO to discuss "what job would make me happy professionally."

I started by telling him, "First, I need you to agree to take me seriously since women are not always taken seriously. I want to submit a bid to purchase the brewery."

There was dead silence on the phone.

I knew Coors did not feel that I could raise the capital. They thought it would only be a matter of time before I walked away.

Why are Deadlines Important?

The bid process had started about a month before I notified Coors of my plans to bid. The first bid milestone required bidders to issue a letter indicating their intent to bid and willingness to comply with the terms of the request for proposal (RFP). They offered me an additional two weeks to prepare this document, but I advised them I would comply with the original RFP deadline. I did not want to start my process asking for exceptions or missing key dates. The tone I set for negotiations communicated that I was professional and could handle complex situations. I expected the other bidder and Coors to comply as well.

I contacted a very close friend, confidant, and legal counsel about the RFP requirements. He sent me to a Memphis law firm that specialized in mergers and acquisitions. We issued the first letter on time with the required language.

The next deadline was tougher than the first. The RFP required bidders to show "proof of funds" to purchase the facility. All banks had turned me down; therefore, I did not have the required financial commitment. The banks either told me "no" or they said nothing in hopes that the RFP timeline would expire. As the deadline approached, I consulted my financial advisor. Long story short, based upon the business plan and his knowledge of my abilities, I was able to get the letter of representation for twenty-five million dollars on time.

Meeting deadlines is critical for securing and maintaining contracts. On my own, I did not possess the knowledge or experience for this type of purchase transaction. I was fortunate to have a network and relationships that could provide legal counsel and guidance throughout the purchase process. My rule: If the other party has legal counsel, you typically need similar representation.

Missing a contract deadline is not a small thing. A missed deadline legally disqualifies you from bidding on a contract. This is true for any contract. I would advise anyone working with time-sensitive contracts to hire professionals to assist you throughout the process. Juggling a multi-million-dollar opportunity and losing it due to timing would be hard to swallow.

Dr. Martin Luther King, Jr., famous pastor, speaker, and author, wrote: "We are now faced with the fact, my friends, that tomorrow is today. We are confronted with the fierce urgency of now. In this unfolding conundrum of life and history, there is such a thing as being too late. Procrastination is still the thief of time. Life often leaves us standing bare, naked, and dejected with a lost opportunity ... Over the bleached bones and jumbled residues of numerous civilizations are written the pathetic words, 'Too late.' ... Now let us begin. Now let us rededicate ourselves to the long and bitter, but beautiful, struggle for a new world."

All I can say to his words is "Amen." If you had an opportunity and lost it due to procrastination or a lack of resources that led you to miss a deadline, accept the fact that you lost that opportunity and pay more respect to deadlines in the future.

How are You Managing Your Life?

In business, time is always in short supply. Entrepreneurs and business owners especially are all juggling too much; therefore, remembering every single appointment is just not going to happen. My mind will drop the memory of an agreed-upon meeting as soon as a new conversation starts. My Outlook manages my life. If it is not in Outlook, it is not going to happen. If someone agrees to meet on a future date, they must send a meeting notice. The most effective nonprofit boards I've worked with send meeting notices months in advance and then send the notice again one week prior as a reminder.

I also have many people reach out who want to meet for coffee to discuss business concerns. My rule is that coffee meetings are scheduled at 7:30 a.m. or 4 p.m. near a highway ramp. Why? Typical business prime time is 9 a.m. to 3 p.m. Prime time is the time you receive the most sales calls and schedule the most business meetings. I protect this prime time as much as possible. Interestingly, most nonprofit boards schedule their meetings between 10 a.m. and 3 p.m. and then wonder why attendance is low or why they can't attract new board members. Nonprofits that do not compensate their board members should avoid scheduling meetings during prime time.

Personally, I use daily planning to maximize each day. I carry a journal so I can note every activity. Each night I list and prioritize all the activities I need to accomplish the next day. During the day, I review my journal to evaluate how my day is progressing compared to what I prioritized the night before. Time management is a top-down strategy. A CEO who is organized and efficient tends to encourage efficiency within the organization. Time is a precious commodity. Once lost, it is gone forever.

There are several strategies managers and leaders can use to manage their own time and respect that of others. Issue an agenda with every meeting. This helps keep the meeting on schedule to respect others' time. Delegation is also critical for time management. Delegation builds employees' capacity and skills while increasing their job satisfaction. The key to effective delegation is choosing a person who has the skills and authority to accomplish the task. The manager must possess good follow-up skills to ensure the task is actually accomplished. Follow-up encourages employees to follow through on the task because they know you will be inspecting what you expect. This optimizes everyone's time while building trust, and employees begin to understand that the manager's job is to get the task done, not necessarily do it themselves.

Open Door Policy

I have an open-door policy with my team, which means my door is always open as when I am not in a meeting. An operational problem is an exception. If a problem occurs in operations, the managers of that department do not have to schedule a meeting. In manufacturing, like many businesses, time is money. If the line is down and employees are standing around, waiting for a decision can be expensive. Based upon your business, it's critical you communicate to employees when it's acceptable to interrupt your closed door. Customers are a priority, but giving the team access to key decision-makers when problems arise communicates your respect and appreciation for employees' contributions.

When I was a manager, employees wanted to linger in my office. I always made it a priority to listen and take notes. Based upon the complexity of the issue, I might schedule a follow-up meeting. Scheduling a specific time to talk about the issue improved preparations and made people confident that issues would be handled in a timely manner. Unscheduled meetings wreak havoc on time management; therefore, planning these meetings keeps you on schedule.

There are of course roles, such as customer service, call centers, and human resources, where availability is required since those roles exist to address unplanned problems. Customers award new business to vendors who respect their business by showing a sense of urgency when it comes to solving their problem. Meeting deadlines despite problems that arise can mean life or death for your business. I encourage professionals to underpromise and overdeliver. We prove the customer is king with our actions, not our words. These roles will likely approach time management differently.

In closing, it is human nature to hate deadlines. To the contrary, I have come to love deadlines because meeting them has kept me in the game when it came to an asset purchase or securing a contract through an RFP process. More importantly, deadlines can be a source of confidence, respect, inspiration, excitement, purpose, and motivation. Managing deadlines, as well as your time in general, is both strategic and critical for the reputation of your business. A business with a reputation of not meeting deadlines will not gain new customers and is destined for failure.

Do you have the all the time in the world?

Not really.

Based upon your reading about "All the Time in the World? Not Really," what actions will you take? Suggestions:

Make a list of opportunities you passed on due to size or complexity. Have you missed an RFP milestone and what caused the delay? What resources would have helped you secure this opportunity?

_____

_____

_____

Review an upcoming opportunity or contract. Develop an action plan to include key steps necessary to execute, assign responsibility, and establish milestones.

_____

_____

_____

List actions for your business to stop in the next year to improve use of time. If you do not already carry a journal, use one for just a month. Evaluate whether your time management and follow-up improved.

_____

_____

_____

Each morning, schedule an uninterrupted hour to review your schedule, plan, and strategize for the business. Evaluate your results from this first hour.

_____

_____

_____

Chapter 6:

Make Up Your Mind

After ten years in accounting at Smucker's, I decided I wanted to change careers and become a plant manager. At the time, there were no women or minorities in Smucker's operations and there were more promotion opportunities in operations than accounting. I had great success in my accounting career, but I had hit the glass ceiling. The challenge was that my knowledge of operations was limited to facilitating the Kepner-Tregoe (KT) process of analyzing operations problems. Kepner-Tregoe is used worldwide across every industry as a problem-solving solution built around a data-driven core that stresses the role of procedure completion in the decision-making process. But I had made up my mind about my career change.

Once I made up my mind, the real work started.

A Closed Mouth Does Not Get Fed

My daughter's favorite saying is: "A closed mouth does not get fed." I needed to share my career ambitions with the right person. I spoke with Smucker's plant manager and COO about my desire for a career in operations. I wanted a career path that would ultimately lead to a plant manager job. Because I had expressed my desire for a career change, after the quality manager was promoted to environmental manager, the COO came to Memphis to offer me the quality manager job. He said this promotion was necessary for me to be considered for a future plant manager opportunity.

The COO needed to know whether I planned to accept or reject the position by Monday. My observation was that everyone respected my plant controller role, but employees had loss respect for the quality manager role. I was concerned that the prior quality manager's practices might overshadow my positive reputation of excitement, inclusion, and accountability. My fear was losing the respect I'd earned as a plant controller. The quality manager position appeared boring with no influence. But I was told I was required to manage quality before I could be promoted to plant manager.

In evaluating the quality manager opportunity, I developed a list of positives and negatives:

Positives	Negatives	Conclusions
Upward mobility	Limited documentation	My written communication skills were very good.
Increased product knowledge	Lack of respect	I was respected by employees at the local plant and throughout the company.
Operations knowledge	Poor reputation	My knowledge of accounting systems and my reputation for timeliness and accuracy resulted in earlier promotions.
Labor relations skills	Lack of structure and process	Accounting timelines and structure is the life of a controller. The accounting team assembles information from many to tell the business story.

Understanding of union environment	Weak support team	I led an amazing team from which other departments would recruit since they knew the quality of my team. In addition, any department we worked with understood their role in maintaining my team's efficiency.

The lists and my conclusions showed me that the ideal candidate for quality manager possessed qualities that matched my strengths. It clearly demonstrated that this was the right opportunity for me.

Never Let a Good Problem Go to Waste!

I never looked back after I had made my decision. People have a tendency to second-guess themselves, wondering if they did the right thing.

> *I have a rule: After I make a decision, I stay focused on my new direction.*

I do not waste time and energy looking back. In order to succeed, I always keep my eye on the new prize. And that's just what I did in my new quality manager position.

I had a reputation of working to address problems that others would avoid. In my mind, there was little to no risk of addressing these problems. The system had failed, and everyone knew it. If the problem was solved, I would be a hero. If my attempt fails, nothing happens. It was already broken. The quality manager role involved establishing polices and procedures to deliver consistent quality, as well as developing training and processes for the entire facility—essentially, tackling problems others had avoided solving.

Choosing Greatness

I'm amazed by how many people talk themselves out of greatness. They have a brilliant idea, but they quickly convince themselves that it will never work. Amazingly, people give fear of failure more power than the enticement of the rewards of success. But you must be the change you wish to see. Tom Collins, author of *Good to Great,* wrote, "Good is the enemy of Great." My mother also hated when things were just "good enough." It takes the same time and energy to strive for greatness as it does to be average.

I always choose greatness.

After I was finally promoted to plant manager from quality manager, the COO asked about my role in decision-making. He said, "Let me be clear. Include your team in the process. They have valuable experience and knowledge and you need buy-in. But, at the end of the day, you are responsible and accountable for all decisions made at your facility." Now I had attorneys at my disposable to provide legal advice, but I was always responsible for the final decision. I had to be a leader with the ability to take input from many people and make decisions. It was a team sport with a single individual catching the heat while the whole team gets the glory.

It is important to get input from others when making decisions. No one person knows everything, nor does anyone expect you to know everything. A manager is expected to use all the resources at their disposal to get the necessary facts prior to making decisions. These resources may be internal, such as employees and peers, or external, such as vendors, suppliers, lawyers, insurance agents, environmentalists, CPAs, or other subject matter experts.

Inclusiveness Drives Profits

Lack of inclusion can be expensive. I once asked a maintenance director about his degree of confidence in his engineering design eliminating the heel dents in cans. He told me there was a 50 percent probability the new design would work. I asked if he had discussed the problem and proposed changes with his maintenance team. He told me he hadn't. His engineers developed the recommendation. I rejected the proposal and insisted that he review the problem and recommendation with his entire team and let them know the recommendation was not final. We needed a solution with a higher probability of success, and that higher probability would come with input from all team members.

Effective leaders must be great listeners who are open to new ideas. They must encourage their team to be open and they must genuinely seek honest input. They must not cut off the conversation and should repeat what they heard to make sure they understood correctly. A leader's actions when seeking input for a decision can either encourage or discourage participation from team members. When the maintenance director asked for feedback from all of his team members, they presented several new options and explained why the revised design would solve the problem and increase probability of success. In the end, the team felt appreciated and respected for their knowledge, and a better decision was made. The tone of the meeting was that solving the problem was more important than who solved it. Engineering proceeded to analyze the recommendation with the equipment manufacturer who agreed that the revised design was more effective. Based upon the higher probability of success, I made up my mind by approving the purchase.

Before finalizing a decision, you should first list the success criteria for that decision. Use those criteria to evaluate whether your solution will meet your objective. Secondly, list the pros and cons of various alternatives, such as costs, risks, timing, resource requirements, constraints, etc. Next, list potential problems associated with each alternative. For each problem, develop a list of contingent actions in the event the problem occurs. If an alternative has a fatal flaw that you cannot solve, reconsider this option. This process ensures your complete understanding of the decision or problem and that you solve the right problems by anticipating potential issues associated with each alternative's execution.

Dangers of Overthinking

There will be times when you must make decisions about things like moving, changing jobs, ending relationships, having surgery, purchasing equipment, or starting a business. The factors and risks of any decision can be so complex that they paralyze people. Leaders must find ways to move past the fear of change, the unknown, and failure. A lot of people are simply more comfortable with status quo and never make any decision at all.

The more you agonize over making decisions, the more confused and stuck you become. Overthinking and compulsively analyzing and re-analyzing a decision doesn't help you make the right one. Trying to predict the future is as impossible as trying to time the stock market. There is risk in anything you do. There is risk regardless of how certain you are about a desired outcome. Life is too unpredictable to know with certainty that you are making the "right" decision. Any decision requires a leap of faith.

Many small businesses just avoid opportunities for significant contracts that appear out of their reach. My approach, as with any decision, is to gather information about the company from the internet or my network. I seek prior contracts, using the Freedom of Information Act, for government contracts to gather information about competitors' service offering and pricing. This information is invaluable to understanding competitors' pricing and terms from the previous bid. Using this information, I develop a proposal to meet or exceed the bid requirements.

With the right amount of information, a decision to move forward can be made.

I once bid on a government contract that others avoided because it involved slow pay, high working capital requirements, and high performance requirements. I built a team qualified to handle the performance requirements, and I planned the working capital budget for the contract considering the slow pay. In evaluating this opportunity, I asked what I had to lose. And after answering this question and making my decision, I started the work, focusing only on what I needed to do to follow through on the decision I made. The bankers handled the line of credit, sales reviewed the proposal, engineering reviewed the plans, and other external relationships contributed to my decision as needed.

Joel Osteen, pastor and author, said, "Make up your mind no matter what comes your way, no matter how difficult, no matter how unfair, you will do more than survive, you will thrive in spite of it."

Making up your mind, whether that decision is to pursue a contract or walk away, is so important. If your business cannot address the potential issues, timelines, quality expectations, or if it cannot deliver services at a competitive price with a reasonable profit, make up your mind to walk away. You have a lot to lose if you choose to pursue an opportunity destined for failure. Failure to perform could impose costly penalties, destroy your credit, or damage your reputation with both new and existing customers. So your decision should not be to go for something by default, but rather make up your mind and stick to your decision regardless of your fear. Trust me, the pain of decision-making is minor compared to the reward of thriving.

Based upon your reading about "Make Up Your Mind," what actions will you take? Suggestions:

Make a list of routine business decisions you made in the past year. Also list whether it was you or another employee who made the decision.

_____

_____

_____

Make a list of decisions that included team members' input.

_____

_____

_____

Make a list of decisions that need to be made in the near future. Assign a team member to each major decision. What outside resources will you need to make that decision? Facilitate an inclusive exercise with employees to discuss.

_____

_____

_____

After six months, evaluate the quality of your decisions using both quantitative measures, such as financial returns and increased sales calls, and qualitative measures, such as employee engagement.

Chapter 7:
Roll Out or Roll Over

A s I stated in earlier chapters, after Coors announced its plans to close the Memphis brewery, I was offered an opportunity to remain with the company. I did not immediately say no, but I recognized that this was my opportunity to evaluate my future. I interviewed with both Anheuser-Busch and Coca-Cola for general manager jobs. The recruiter I worked with was impressed with my management experience in a union environment. Both companies were seeking a change manager with strong labor relations, communications, and leadership skills and were impressed and interested after my contract with Coors ended. But I was confident in my ability to excel with a new opportunity; therefore, I decided to roll out instead of rolling over in my existing profession.

What does it mean to roll out and roll over? When someone rolls over, it means they stop resisting or examining a decision for themselves and they do what someone else wants them to do. Rolling over can also occur when you simply stay the course and resist change or a challenge. Most people and organizations just roll over and give up when they're challenged or attacked. Rolling out requires you to make a decision to either leave or find new solutions. The problem or concern with which you are presented might violate a contract, be insurmountable, or lack integrity to the point that you decide to end the contract, challenge the decision, or discontinue the relationship. Rolling out also occurs when you refuse to stay the course by finding new options that can deliver your desired outcome.

Rolling Out

I knew I had exceptional leadership skills, and I was still impressed by the number of job opportunities that were offered to me. However, I felt like it was time for me to start a business. Clearly, I had the knowledge, skills, resilience, energy, and passion that business ownership requires. The only other characteristic I needed was the courage to leave my career. As my confidence in my abilities continued to grow, I asked myself: Should I start Hardy Bottling or stay with my comfortable job in Corporate America? I had to decide if I was going to roll out of my comfort zone or roll over and stay my current course.

I spoke with my family about my ambitions. I reviewed my preliminary plans and told them why the timing was perfect for my career change. I had their full support. It was time to act.

My family and I were investing over 50 percent of our wealth, giving up a comfortable executive job with bonus and stock options. This career change really required me to understand my "why." Why did I want a career change? What business was I interested in pursuing? How would I make it happen? Where do I start? My mind was racing all the time, even when my outer appearance was calm.

The Challenges of Rolling Out

Roll out or roll over can take on many faces and forms. It occurs frequently in business situations, not just personal career decisions. For example, when a customer refuses to pay for services, a supplier has two options. One is to file a lawsuit against the customer. The other is to find a workable solution. I was once asked by a customer to make a machine modification in order to package a special twelve-pack carton. After two months, we completed the machine conversion. The customer was invoiced but refused to pay. So, I met with my team to discuss the situation and develop our options.

Now this was our largest customer. The pack fees covered our monthly operating costs. The change parts cost over 100,000 dollars while our monthly revenue was over 300,000 dollars. As we discussed our options to recover our cost, suing was never a consideration. I discussed the situation with the customer's business development manager who had authorized the equipment conversion. I said, "I understand you are not going to reimburse Hardy for the conversion."

He said his boss would not authorize payment.

As an alternative, I requested approval to purchase corn syrup for Hardy to resell to our customers to recover our cost for the conversion.

He authorized one car a month. We ordered two cars a month, figuring it would be three or four months before they stopped sending cars. The customer's corn syrup cost was 15,000 dollars cheaper per car than my cost.

At the end of the six months, we had earned over 200,000 dollars on corn syrup sales.

You could say I rolled over and did nothing when that customer refused to pay, but I say I rolled out. I refused to stay the course by finding an option that delivered value exceeding my cost. This was a win-win while lawsuits would have been a lose-lose.

Suing a customer rarely results in a good outcome. In the end, it does not matter if you are right and the customer is wrong. If I had sued, it would have been an example of winning the battle but losing the war. After a lawsuit, customer–supplier relationship is never the same. In most cases, the outcome includes the loss of a valuable customer. In addition to the public relations fallout, your reputation as a supplier of suing customers may impact your ability to attract new customers. The ideal customer and supplier have a seamless relationship in which they complement each other. A lawsuit only should occur when two parties cannot find an equitable solution. I recommend finding a solution that adds value to your bottom line. This will require creative thinking from both parties, but it is possible. The key is letting level heads, not emotions, prevail.

When to Roll Out

When should you roll out or roll over? There is no perfect answer. This decision will be different for each business situation. As a rule, I recommend you meet with the customer to discuss why they are not paying. Discuss options for you to recover your costs, such as returning equipment or supplies. Suing customers is not free and, in most cases, the only winners will be the lawyers.

You can also look at the value of the customer. How much did this customer cost you? Is it cheaper to cease providing services? All customers are not good customers. The customer is not always right, but the secret is focusing on how you communicate and resolve differences rather than on which party is right.

Regardless, a meeting with the customer to discuss the problem is the best initial course of action. If the customer is having financial problems, work out a payment schedule. If the customer needs supplies in the future, a prepaid arrangement could create a win-win. I have been the customer behind on payments. My suppliers were willing to accept payment terms when I was low on working capital, and my honesty and willingness to work with my vendors created a solid long-term relationship.

If the customer is unresponsive after repeated attempts to collect payment, you have several final options. The last option before suing should always be another attempt to obtain payment. This can be accomplished by sending a final demand letter from a lawyer or collection agency to the customer. In most instances, a final demand letter is successful. Typically, it only takes that one demand letter to receive payment. But, if the first letter does not work, I would recommend you try one last time before setting a lawsuit in motion. If the customer does not respond to your final requests for payment, you can write off the bad debt, send it to a debt collection agency, or prepare to take legal action. You can file a lawsuit to recover your liability in small claims or civil trial court.

Debt collection is another method to collect claims that is less intrusive than a lawsuit. Debt collection agencies act as middlemen, collecting customer's delinquent debts. Debts must be at least sixty days past due and the creditor pays the collector a substantial percentage, typically 25 to 45 percent of the amount collected. Debt collection agencies collect delinquent debts of all types. For difficult-to-collect debts, collection agencies negotiate settlements and may refer cases to lawyers who can then file a lawsuit. Using debt collection or selling the receivables to a factoring agency cleans the supplier's hands since they do not control the tactics of the factoring or collection agency.

When You Must Sue

Sixty percent of the claims filed in small claims court are filed by businesses.[6] Small claims courts have limited jurisdiction. The parties do not need to be represented by an attorney. Small claims courts are limited to resolving simple disputes quickly and economically for dollar amounts ranging from 1,500 to 25,000 dollars, depending on the state. The procedures are informal. In small claims court, the judgment is usually rendered immediately after the hearing. My experience has been that once a court date is set, the customer will most likely attempt to settle the debt.

Suing in civil trial court is a different animal. The parties must hire an attorney, and the debt exceeds the limited amount of a small claims court. A lawsuit in civil court follows complicated rules and procedures. It is also more expensive to pursue an action in civil trial court. As I mentioned earlier, it is possible that the mere filing of a lawsuit against a customer for nonpayment will induce them to offer to settle the debt, which would be the best outcome.

The Right Way to Roll Out

I once attended a dinner at which a business owner discussed problems she was having with a client. The client was a large employer in a large metropolitan area. Her client requested background information on the temporary employees assigned to their facility. She did not think it was legal to provide the information; therefore, she ignored the request. Rather than discussing her concerns with the client, she gave the client's administrator the runaround. That administrator retaliated with delaying payment by 120 days versus the normal thirty days. When the business owner complained about the administrator's actions, she was immediately paid, but she lost the relationship. She did not roll over, but I am concern she will be rolled out against her will.

This business owner could have taken several courses of action. The first problem was that she was limited by what she knew. She understood her company's responsibility to protect employees' records, but she did not know the client's requirements or their authority to review temporary staff records. The information requirements for organizations receiving federal funds differ from others. Both parties were right, but no one was communicating. If both sides had communicated and explained their concerns, the relationship loss would have been avoided. Communicating provides an opportunity for each party to understand the other's needs and limitations. Instead, a relationship was lost forever.

I value my customers, and they value me. If we get the communication and value right, the relationship will weather most storms. The goal is for the customer to view your services as the gold standard and only think of your company to provide those services. If a customer owes you money, contact the owner or president for a personal conversation. Offer the same courtesy and thoughtfulness as when you were courting them as a customer. Roll over or roll out handled right helps you win the battle—and the war. Rolling over requires that you give up and accept the status quo, resulting in a win-lose that eventually may result in you rolling out. On the other hand, rolling out means that you seek creative solutions and options that create a win-win and maintain a valuable relationship.

Based upon your reading about "Roll Out or Roll Over," what actions will you take? Suggestions:

What are your credit terms and what are your customers' requirements? How can you meet them without bankrupting the company?

_____

_____

_____

Review your customer contracts. Based upon your learning, list all provisions that you would change to improve your outcome–to win the battle _and_ the war.

_____

_____

_____

Make a list of customers who consistently pay invoices late. Are they good customers? Schedule a meeting to discuss future payment plans. What do you have to lose?

_____

_____

_____

Update your customer contract template in the following areas: pricing, service expectations, payment terms, and what's included in the contract.

_____

_____

_____

Chapter 8:

Timing is Everything

Eight months after launching Henderson Transloading, a major grain company offered me a million-dollar contract to provide transloading services. They required those services to start within a set deadline of fourteen weeks. My first customer owned all the equipment we were using at the time; therefore, that equipment could not be used for the new customer. This new customer was ten times larger than my existing customer, and my only constraint was getting the equipment on time.

We decided to purchase and install our own equipment to service this new contract. The equipment had a standard eight-week lead time, but we had a four-week deadline at that point. The equipment vendor bids were very close. Both brands were industry leaders. Therefore, the equipment vendor that could meet the deadline would win the contract. I scheduled a meeting with each vendor to discuss the bid and lead time.

First, I met with the vendor with the lowest bid to ensure its costs included installation. I told him the deal was contingent upon equipment delivery in less than four weeks and he told me that four weeks was impossible. I responded by telling him that, based on my experience, I knew that many companies delay delivery of equipment if their site is not ready. I asked him to call his manufacturer to ask if another customer had pushed back a delivery date. If so, I suggested he tell them that he needed the unit and they could build another for the customer who pushed back the delivery date. I told him this sell was contingent upon early delivery. And I made the same offer to the second bidder. Later that day, the lowest bidder confirmed he could deliver the equipment in less than four weeks. As I predicted, another company had delayed delivery. They won the contract.

Recognizing the Opportunity

My success in life has occurred for two reasons: I am either smart or lucky. Most days I need a combination of both. Being in the right place at the right time is not good enough. You must be in the right place at the right time *and* know what to do with the opportunity.

For that customer who was scheduling a heavy equipment move with an expensive crane, timing is everything. By delaying the equipment delivery, that customer avoided paying for the crane twice. It was a financial benefit for that customer to delay delivery. And because they made a decision about timing, we secured a major grain contract by doing the impossible. This contract was valued at one million dollars per year. Our plan B was to lease the unit at 10 percent of the cost of a new unit, which was nonrefundable. It was a viable option. But it was a better option to meet the customer's timeline using out-of-the-box thinking at the best possible cost.

A contractual deadline creates momentum with a sense of urgency. When I wanted to dismantle a packaging line and move it to a new location, Coors's engineers said it would take nine months, but the COO wanted production to resume in three months to avoid backorders. The timing was critical because this line was the only plastic production line in the U.S. for Coors. Therefore, missing startup would cause shortages throughout the United States.

I told the COO that if engineering controlled the project, it would take nine months, but my team would meet the three-month deadline if we were allowed to control it. We approached the project with a detailed plan and a sense of urgency with no constraints or concern when it came to budget. You can often make faster progress on a time-constrained project by rescheduling low priority tasks so you can utilize these resources for the time-constrained project. Other ways to maneuver around time constraints include working overtime, assigning work to other team members, or even outsourcing the project. Of course, all of those involve financial cost, and that financial cost is often the trade-off for accomplishing a time-constrained project.

When the COO again challenged me on whether the reduced timeline was possible, I told him the RFP for the project set a two-and-a-half month deadline with contractors working seven days a week, twenty-four hours a day. The contractors were motivated since the contract imposed significant penalties if the deadline was missed.

This project ended up being a huge success. The contractors meet the deadline. The production line test was successful, and the production of high-quality products resumed. Timing was everything for this project and my career.

Making It Happen

In order to meet this deadline, the contractors developed a detailed plan with key steps and timelines for accomplishing each major milestone. The plan allowed different subcontractors to perform many tasks simultaneously. This was the type of project that could have ended my career if it had gone badly, but I was not worried because my timeline included a cushion.

A time-constrained project also requires close monitoring of details. Each week, we reviewed the project status with the contractor. If the timeline was off, the contractor was required to add resources to bring it back on schedule. This was a no-excuses project. I did not put restrictions on how they did it. They simply had to get it done.

We held daily project meetings. I required total honesty about problems that could impede progress and project status. Problems were accepted and expected, but lies were not. We could not solve what we did not know. Any obstacles were immediately discussed and resolved. We could not afford to lose hours or days because a contractor was waiting on something or someone. For example, if the contractor needed a line down for eight hours to make a connection, we changed the schedule to accommodate that need. We caught up on lost production later with overtime.

This project also could not afford turf wars. The only enemy was not completing this project on time. My open-door policy and management-by-walking-around style were well-known.

I would walk up to the contractor and ask about the project status. I did not accept excuses about anything. Everyone had access to me, the key decision-maker. Walking around was another way to provide access for those not comfortable coming to my office. The goal was to minimize risk to the project by increasing communication and inclusiveness.

> *If you want hourly employees to speak freely,*
> *meet them on their turf.*

Timing is critical with everything you do. Luck is appreciated, but a detailed plan is better insurance. We only have twenty-four hours in a day, and time lost cannot be recovered. The challenges of work–life balance are real. I manage my time using these simple steps:

1. I start every day with a clear focus.

I make a to-do list to ensure I focus on the right priorities. I know a major problem can derail me; therefore, this list is a reminder of all the priorities that must be accomplished. I review my to-do in the morning while I am having my first cup of coffee.

2. I manage my to-do list.

Remember, the to-do list is a tool, and you are the boss. I meet people who spend so much time with their to-do list that I am sure the list is managing them. Manage your to-do list to prevent emergencies or emotions managing you. My to-do list is prepared the day prior and updated throughout the day. I use notations such as "H" for high priority. These are usually tasks with a high value to the business, that remove an obstacle causing trouble for project team, or that are critical to customer satisfaction. I use "C" for complete or closed and "F/U" for follow-up and detail what follow-up is needed and the person's name. These notations provide status and follow-up information at a glance.

3. I minimize interruptions and disruptions.

When I was a VP for Honeywell, the coders could not be efficient if they were constantly interrupted. If the client interrupted them, it was usually to instruct them to work on lower priorities or even change the scope of the project. The client would then be upset when the original schedule was not met, and my team would be discouraged after working extra hours but remaining behind schedule. Therefore, I required the client to discuss the project with me, the project manager. If the client requested a scope change, it needed to be documented and signed off by the customer project manager and me. I would present the cost of the scope change and the impact on the project timing. This was a politically correct way of letting the customer know that his team caused the delay. The efficiency and the quality of my team's work skyrocketed, as well as their job satisfaction. The constant interruptions and frequent scope changes only created frustration, resulting in loss of focus. Plan your day to allow for time to return calls, handle email, plan the next day, and think strategically and creatively. Everybody deserves a little uninterrupted time to think, reflect, and create.

4. I believe I can.

Henry Ford notably said, "Whether you think you can, or think you can't, you're correct." Your mindset impacts your ability to thrive and a positive attitude helps you find ways to solve complex problems. A negative mindset creates a self-fulfilling prophecy that you cannot win. Walt Disney said that the coolest way to get off the ground is to stop talking and call for action. My team at Honeywell wanted to stop talking, focus, and write code as well as they believed they could.

5. I review each day.

At the end of every day I review the day's activities while my mind is fresh. I update my to-do list, send any last-minute emails about what I will need the next day, and send notes on any follow-ups. This review sets up the next day to be efficient and effective.

Timing can turn an idea or opportunity into a huge success, such as the expedited equipment purchase for transloading that resulted in a one-million-dollar contract. On the other hand, bad timing can destroy an otherwise successful career, such as if there had been a delay in relocating the plastic bottle line.

In business, timing is everything. Unfortunately, many people think good timing is just luck. Nothing could be further from the truth. Meeting aggressive deadlines requires planning, aggressive project management, open lines of communication, a capable team, creative thinking, and a no-excuses approach to success. Timing is a critical success factor, and you can learn to use it to your advantage ... or let it destroy your business. The ability to handle complex situations with tight schedules can give you an incredible competitive advantage.

My rule is: When you put your reputation on the line to meet a deadline, put your best on the line. Your best team members are usually willing to sacrifice the time and emotional energy necessary to win. There is a difference in confidence levels between "It may happen" and "It's going to happen." It's going to happen because of your ability to plan, organize, and execute time–constrained projects and flexibility that allows you to efficiently address high-priority customer needs. The goal is to be branded as the go-to vendor in a crisis because they know you understand that timing is everything.

Based upon your reading about "Timing is Everything," what actions will you take? Suggestions:

Make a list of customers or opportunities you lost because of an inability to meet timing or create a list of contracts you desire but do not have. List the date each contract will expire.

_____

_____

_____

Start keeping a journal of your day-to-day activities. List changes to manage your day. After a month, evaluate whether you are more efficient.

_____

_____

_____

Can timing create a competitive advantage? Make a list of the potential advantages of being able to tackle time-constrained projects.

_____

_____

_____

List ways to gain information about upcoming contract opportunities that may be time-constrained. Use the Freedom of Information Act when applicable. Schedule lunch with procurement officers to ask specific questions. The worst anyone can say is "no."

_____

_____

_____

Chapter 9:

The Secret Sauce to Good PR

After only two years in business, my first company, Hardy Bottling, was hit by an F4 tornado. The brewery, which consists of twenty-nine acres under roof, sustained fifty million dollars in damages, which was significantly higher than my twenty-five-million-dollar insurance limit.

What could I do to save my employees, customers, and reputation?

That disaster caused me to question my ability to recover. What would my customers think? How would I retain them during this process? It was during this time that I first appreciated the role of public relationships. Alan Harrington, writer and professional footballer, writes, "Public-relations specialists make flower arrangements of the facts, placing them so the wilted and less attractive petals are hidden by sturdy blooms." Public relations (PR) control why, when, what, how, and where information is shared with the public to raise awareness—and to create a positive image for Hardy Bottling during a not-so-positive time.

The Campaign

John Lister's article titled "Three Characteristics of a Public Relations Campaign" states: "Ultimately a public relations campaign has three characteristics:
- identifying an objective,
- finding the message that will help achieve that objective, and
- communicating that message to the appropriate audience."[7]

Hardy's PR campaign objective was to retain customers while rebuilding by providing timely updates on the brewery recovery activities. In the short-term, customers are compassionate, but concern for lost production of their brand would determine their future actions. Therefore, our message was crafted to include specific information about our recovery timeline. We provided both written and verbal communication at planned intervals.

This successful campaign required mastery of several skills: excellent written and verbal communication skills, exceptional attention to detail, emotional intelligence, and effective use of the media.

Effective communications are your best friend when saving your business. And those communications must connect with the targeted audience. Therefore, you must know who is receiving the message and understand their concerns. Communications to employees, customers, or the community must adhere to the three Bs: Be Brief, Be Bright, and Be Gone. The speech must be polished and concise. Avoid rambling, jokes, or off-cuff remarks. Maintain eye contact with the audience and do not fidget so that you communicate confidence with sincerity. Written communication is equally important. Your message must be crystal clear and appropriate for a broader audience. Always assume the message can be leaked to others without approval. Social media can share your confidential message in seconds.

In this situation, attention to detail was also critical to ensure that every contract, insurance policy, and legal requirement was compliant. After the tornado, the attorney reviewed all of our contracts to make sure we understood our liability for the customer's products, and the insurance broker confirmed our policy limitations.

Luckily, we did not experience any contract or compliance issues, but when businesses must own up to those issues, their messaging must explain the situation truthfully but to the benefit of the company. What you say, how you say it, and when you say it goes a long way. Sooner is always better than later.

> *Bad news is not like a fine wine; it does not get better with age.*

The business that reveals the concern before it leaks leaves their customers and the community feeling like they are both honest and transparent. The customer and community that receive information from others first suspect a cover-up, which results in a loss of trust. We notified our customers to advise their insurance companies of the loss caused by the tornado and told them we would provide documentation to support their insurance claims.

Effective PR gives attention to details to minimize concerns about the company. The PR communication's message and the company's actions create goodwill to avoid a PR nightmare or risk tarnishing the company's reputation. For example, our communications and support of our customers' insurance claims was our way of letting the customers know that the contract did not cover insurance claims for product losses.

Emotional Intelligence

After any unexpected event or disaster, emotions run high for employees, family members, customers, and the general public. These emotions must be controlled in order to achieve the desired objective of a PR campaign. Therefore, emotional intelligence (EI) is fundamental to developing an effective PR campaign.

Having EI means being aware of emotion driving behavior and impacting people both positively and negatively. It means learning to manage both your own emotions and those of others, especially under pressure. Someone possessing EI can recognize, understand, and manage their own emotions and recognize, understand, and influence the emotions of others. Some people naturally possess EI, but it is a skill you can practice and develop. The best way to practice improving emotionally intelligent behavior is to put yourself in complex situations where you understand how you should behave or respond. Stick to this understood behavior regardless of how uncomfortable you feel until you become comfortable. With enough practice, your brain will adapt to the new behaviors and replace bad EI behaviors.

The news of the tornado hitting Hardy made national news. My children and customers were aware of the disaster. My children were devastated and in tears. They wanted to understand God's message. They asked, "Mom, you have worked harder than anyone we know. How can He expect you to bear more?" I told them to trust that God has a plan. I wanted to sleep and think and pray for the strength to trust His plan.

The next day, Hardy Bottling was a war zone. Debris was everywhere with policemen blocking the streets. We had to hire armed guards to patrol the facility. The building had a foot of standing water and over 300,000 square feet of roof missing. The cars were destroyed in the parking lots. I walked around looking at two years of my life gone in sixty seconds. The voice in the back of my mind asked, "What now?"

Several days after the tornado, a friend who was a CEO at a major company called to inquire about my mental state. I answered, "This is like a funeral at which your children are emotional and Mom must show strength and a positive disposition. The truth is, I have been to hell and back—twice!"

You see, public relations required me to remain positive and lead from a position of strength. For the moment, hell and negative emotions had to stay in my pocket, out of sight.

I asked my management team, "What do you want to do?"

They asked, "What do you mean?"

"Do you want to play or quit?"

"We will do whatever you want."

"I want to play."

They said they would play as long as I believed we could win, and I told them it would be hard, but I had the right team to win. And we got to work.

First, we set up a communication strategy to save our customers and employees. We controlled the messages to customers. The messages were always upbeat with time-specific updates for recovery completion. We appreciated when customers expressed concern but also understood their brands were at risk. They needed answers or, at minimum, a plan.

We had fifty customers to contact. The strategy was to speak to each customer to reassure them that Hardy was still in business. Our communication was sent to our PR firm (two or three outlined paragraphs) to ensure the message had the desired impact. The first message, though brief, was factual, time-bound, positive, and upbeat. The manager delivering the message had the least knowledge about our operations recovery so that if a customer did pry for additional information, they would not expect her to have the answer with her role in sales.

I personally called our top ten customers who together made up 80 percent of our gross revenue. The message points were the same. I was upbeat, stating that our employees were safe, and thanked them for their prayers. I talked about what they wanted to hear: a commitment to provide specific recovery plans in ten days. I understood that our customers' brands were at risk and that it takes months to qualify a bottler. After each call, I sent the same letter we used for our smaller customers for our larger customers to use in their internal distributions. Busy CEOs need tools to tell your story right. I knew they would take the most efficient approach and use my summary. Remember, you always want to control the message.

A Team Sport

Another key to our successful recovery was the team assuming new roles and responsibilities focused on rebuilding. This allowed for greater attention to detail. Trusting your team allows you to divide and conquer. Employees needed information to be effective in this new role, and we shared the details about our insurance limitations while establishing spending rules. First, safety repairs were performed, then repairs required for government or customer regulations.

The leadership team displayed emotional intelligence (EI) by putting their game faces on and being especially sensitive to employees' concerns. This game face remained in place while clearing the grounds of debris in order to control the public and customer perception of the extent of damage. Emotional intelligence helped control how we appeared to employees and customers. Even the colors of my clothes were used to convey positive messages. I wore bright colors and displayed happy body language to communicate confidence and a positive attitude. When communicating compassion, facts, and sad messages, I wore dark colors, made eye contact, and displayed posed body language. After the tornado, I always wore bright colors, remained very positive, and never looked tired—thanks to makeup.

I was told many times that Hardy Bottling would not recover. Many advised me to give up like any self-respecting American should: Take your money and stay home. The insurance company said that over 80 percent of sole proprietorships hit by a tornado with this level of damage closed shop. The statistics were against me, but they always have been. I kept telling everyone we were going to recover.

It's amazing how businesses get written off before we even get started with recovery. Competitors called offering to service my customers. The price of contract bottling increased 20 percent at the prospect of me being out of the game, which would have created a capacity shortage in the industry.

But our second written communication was issued in ten days as planned. We assured customers that Hardy Bottling would resume manufacturing on a set date. After the written communication, I called each customer to thank them for their prayers and patience. Effective PR involves sharing a positive message and attitude that instill trust and confidence. I explained how the facility was being repaired and by whom along with the specific recovery dates.

A great PR professional knows that the media can be friend or foe. We invited the media to join our celebration and witness Hardy Bottling reopening and resuming production. We also issued a final written communication to all customers announcing this accomplishment with a link to the media articles. Remember, people believe what they read—especially on the internet!

Warren Buffet says, "It takes 20 years to build a reputation and five minutes to ruin it. If you think about that, you'll do things differently." This represents the impact of my journey. It took over twenty years for me to gain enough experience and knowledge and sixty seconds for the tornado to take it away. I have spent my life taking my life back, and this was no different. This challenge just required controlling others' perceptions and emotions about our ability to recover.

Effective public relations were the secret sauce to saving Hardy Bottling. Business owners must communicate with their team, customers, and community in both good and bad times. Leaders must make sure every positive message is repeated over and over again. All news must be carefully scripted, and the right person must deliver it at the right time, practicing the three Bs. Remember, customers hate surprises. And if you want to get a message to a broad audience, tell the person who cannot keep a secret, draft an elevator speech for the team, and remember that the press is your friend. Great PR makes each customer feel they are the best ever. What the tornado took away, the secret sauce of PR brought back.

Based upon your reading about "The Secret Sauce to Good PR," what actions will you take? Suggestions:

Write out your company's public relations goals. What would you do if you were hit by a tornado or other disaster?

_____

_____

_____

Who is your targeted audience? What do you know about them? What do you want them to know about your business?

_____

_____

_____

List strategies, regardless of cost, that could accomplish your PR objectives.

_____

_____

_____

Schedule a meeting with a PR firm and request a proposal. How do they measure success? This information will be invaluable.

_____

_____

_____

Chapter 10:

The Power in People

Remember when company loyalty resulted in thirty, or even forty, years of service with the same organization? This was a source of pride for our grandparents. Companies would host ceremonies to award the traditional gold watch to employees who retired after thirty to fifty years of service.

These were employees who believed in the mission of the organization. That bond of loyalty between a company and its employees caused them to place the needs of the other ahead of the bottom line, family, and self. My father, like so many others of his generation, tells stories of the company placing the employee's needs ahead of profits or the company caring for a team member with an unexpected disability or other complex situations.

Today, these stories are few and far between. Most of us think of these stories as the "good ole days" or our grandparents' stories—nothing that applies in the workplace today.

Employee Relations

At Smucker's, a temporary layoff was required every fall because of insufficient sales coupled with improved operational efficiency. Production only ran three to four days a week. Historically, junior employees were laid off during this time, allowing senior employees to work five days each week. But I was concerned that it was the junior employees with young families who could least afford a pay cut. One year, we decided all employee hours would be equally reduced to equalize earnings. At first, the senior employees complained, but seeing the junior employees' positive reactions caused senior employees to accept the new system. This positive peer pressure placed the greater good ahead of self. The change in balancing hours created a more unified workforce. They were all in it together.

Our goal was to grow the business enough for all employees to earn forty hours' pay during this slower season. The first year, we deferred all employee training to the fall season, utilizing that seasonal downtime. This eliminated the need to reduce employee hours. My facility was the first to implement world-class strategies such as quality at the source, operator changeovers, and operator's equipment overhaul, and this required many hours of training for all employees.

After training employees to change over equipment, we eliminated subcontractor hours. The employee changeover team replaced subcontractors during annual equipment overhauls. They had the responsibility of breaking down the equipment, which increased employee hours. This newfound work strategy between operators and mechanics had the added bonus of improving relationships. The changeover operator was "the Nurse" since they prepared the machine by taking it apart and cleaning it. The mechanic ("the Doctor") would troubleshoot and replace parts. The operator would later reassemble the machine and test it. Startup after the changeover was the most efficient in the history of the company with this new work strategy, and that accomplishment improved morale and company loyalty.

Similar to Smucker's, employees at Hardy Bottling were self-directed and embraced quality at the source. I trusted them to manage the customer's business as if it were their own. They understood that their success was tied to the business's success. They adhered to customer specifications, challenged unclear or unreasonable instructions, and documented exceptions. My employees were highly skilled. When you think about employee relations, you have to keep in mind that as a business owner, you are entrusting the millions of dollars you invest to individual employees' decisions.

Hiring Family

Herschel Walker, famous NFL player, says that hiring the wrong team was his number one mistake in his business. This problem was destroying his company while negatively impacting family relationships. You see, he had hired family members to build his business team but soon learned that was a major mistake. If family members are brought on board, they must approach business with the same values, passion, and integrity as the owner. Other employees see family members' failures as the owner's failure. Herschel's family members arrived late and left early, and work results were an afterthought. This impacted the momentum and attitude of non-family team members. His family members' values became the values of his team, and Herschel ultimately had to terminate family members to save his business. When he did that, it not only sent a message but also improved his relationship with his team. When it comes to hiring family members, proceed with caution.

Customer Relations

One time at Hardy Bottling, we were producing a product for a new customer. The recipe had no special instructions, nor did the formulator flag sensitive ingredients. Employees followed the recipe instructions to the letter. The customer supplied the tray, which we discovered was formed backwards. We notified the customer about the defect and offered to use a substitute tray, but the customer directed management to make every effort to run the defective tray.

Three hours later, the customer approved the substitute tray.

But a week later, the liquid developed an odor of a rotten egg. It was not fit for consumption. The customer claimed we ruined their liquid and demanded reimbursement. We told them the problem was under investigation. The truth was that we did not know why the odor occurred.

The third-party formulator claimed the recipe was not the issue, and our investigation identified a new ingredient. We contacted the ingredient manufacturer to ask if the ingredient required special handling. They said to avoid excess heat during production or the product develops a rotten egg odor. The product had been hot for over three hours in the defective tray, which was provided by the customer.

I discussed the problem with another expert. He said the same defect occurred a few months earlier with him and another co-packer. He reimbursed this same customer for the loss. Then a month later, this same customer hired a new formulator and Hardy Bottling without disclosing the previous problem.

I notified the customer of our findings and told them we would not reimburse the cost. The customer had not provided us with special instructions and the downtime in their production was the result of their defective tray. We terminated the contract and instructed them to pick up all materials. The decision to terminate the relationship was based on two premises. The first was that we could not trust this customer and the second was that the formula's narrow tolerance was too sensitive.

We were firm but respectful in our communications. My rule is to always be professional while providing clear, concise data or directions. The data should include facts, expert information, and pictures, if possible. The facts in this case minimized negative discussions and allowed us to roll them out when they expected Hardy Bottling to roll over.

The foundation of customer–client relations is trust. When information is supplied from a reputable source, you assume that information is accurate. The goal is a seamless relationship. The customer should have your back and you should have theirs for an optimal outcome. Trust is a fundamental rule of engagement. Some rules are more like guidelines for us, but the broken trust rule ends the relationship for my businesses. This customer was looking for a scapegoat, and Hardy was not it.

In another look at customer relations, I have a long-term relationship with a supplier whose pride and integrity drove the culture of his company. My relationship with U.S. Bottlers spans over thirty years, starting when I worked for the J. M. Smucker Company. They installed the first plastic bottle capper at Smucker's to produce sundae syrup. I experienced U.S. Bottlers's integrity and reputation when they decided to re-engineer and rebuild a three-year-old capper. U.S. Bottlers was not satisfied with their older capper's performance, and the rebuilt machine's performance was exceptional. There was no finger pointing between customer and supplier. U.S. Bottlers was not proud of the performance of their machine and accepted the responsibility of resolving it. They valued integrity over bottom line. And, in the long run, integrity improves the business bottom line.

I was awarded a contract from Coca-Cola that required Hardy Bottling to build a new hot fill packaging system. The new system, which included flash pasteurizer, filler, capper, labelers, packers, and line modifications, cost over six million dollars. Our working capital could only support a five-million-dollar capital plan. We met with U.S. Bottlers's CEO and manager to discuss the project cost overrun and explained our financial dilemma. This project was critical to our success since this was a fast-growing category. The contract with Coca-Cola would stabilize our business. U.S. Bottlers sells new fillers, but they understood my limited capital. This was a special filler; therefore, buying a cheaper model was not an option. However, they did recommend we purchase a used filler and rebuild it. They located a used filler and rebuilt it, and they also provided a new filler warranty with it. This filler was the most reliable equipment on our new line. The final cost of the rebuilt filler solution was 170,000 dollars, significantly lower than the 1.2 million dollars a new filler would have cost.

What is the value of relationships? Although we could crunch some numbers from the last example, I have learned that relationships are priceless. The equipment vendor willing to rebuild a machine to save my business demonstrated the power of a long-term relationship. Business owners must give employees authority and trust them to do the job. And the customer is always right until they are not. It was my responsibility as the supplier to provide detailed information to refute the customer's claim of negligence when they provided us with a defective tray.

In the "good ole days," my father worked as a truck driver for a plumbing supply company for over thirty years. The company supported my father through ups and downs. He never experienced a temporary layoff or downsizing. The company understood that success requires employees' past, current, and future contributions. If companies want loyal employees, they must be a loyal employer; it's that simple. Employers must understand the contribution of loyalty to the bottom line. The value of loyalty is priceless. Maybe what businesses need today is to understand what their forefathers knew: The power is in the people and relationships.

**Based upon your reading about "The Power in People,"
what actions will you take? Suggestions:**

Think about your business. List the characteristics of your ideal team. Now document the strengths and weaknesses of your current team.

_____

_____

_____

What is your relationship with customers like? Make a list of good relationships and a list of those needing improvement.

_____

_____

_____

Compare and contrast your worst and best customer relationship. Make a list of characteristics or tasks that contribute to each. List specific actions you can take to move the worst to best.

_____

_____

_____

Make a list of missed opportunities over the past month to improve your relationships with employees.

_____

_____

_____

Chapter 11:

Sell with Heart

A while ago, Apple had an advertisement: "Here's to the Crazy Ones, Think Different." This advertising slogan challenged consumers to never be afraid to "Think Different." When Hardy Bottling got up and running, we only utilized about 10 percent of our production capacity.

We needed more customers.

Initially I thought of all beverage co-packers in the U.S. as our competitors. But after "thinking differently," we offered our co-packer services to other co-packers who could not produce newer packages that Hardy already had equipment for. Therefore, when their customers needed services outside their capabilities, the co-packer called us and became our customer. We worked for the co-packer, who was able to maintain his valuable customer relationship.

Understand Your Target Audience

The key to selling is understanding the target audience to help them understand your value proposition and "think differently" with you.

When I started Hardy Bottling, I pursued PepsiCo as a customer to manufacture energy drinks and other specialty products. Pepsi's portfolio of specialty products made them a good prospect for offering my co-packing services. We researched their beverage portfolio's product specifications to evaluate capability within our operation. We confirmed that our process would produce a comparable product. I contacted Pepsi's diversity manager to discuss my facility capabilities and background. I told them we had the experience to produce high-quality beverages. As a former VP for Coors Brewing Company, this was not rocket science … so I thought.

After speaking with Pepsi's diversity manager, he indicated he would review our presentation and capability statement. He agreed to contact me within two weeks to discuss it further. After waiting a month, I tried to contact him to discuss the opportunity. I called him for over three months at different times of the day to try to catch him when he was available.

I got lucky when he answered my call after 5 p.m. one of those times.

I quickly identified myself and asked if he had any questions about our capabilities. I wanted to pursue co-packing opportunities with Pepsi. He was irritated that he had answered the phone. He was rude and told me he would not put his career on the line for a new co-packer. I thanked him for his time and ended the call.

I was hurt by his rejection but not crushed. This was Pepsi's lost, not Carolyn Hardy's or Hardy Bottling. Pepsi did not reject Carolyn Hardy, the top professional, former VP for Coors; it rejected the risk—and reward—of working with a new beverage manufacturer. The key to maintaining professionalism is to always remember that it's about the business, not you the individual. You must keep this in mind in order to sell with your heart while not allowing rejection to break it.

A year later, on behalf of the chamber of commerce, I was meeting with a woman whose company was considering expansion to Memphis. We were discussing her new rubber tire shedding business, and she asked if I manufactured for PepsiCo. I said no, and I told her I wanted to know why she asked. It turns out, she was on the diversity advisory committee for Pepsi. The committee had asked Pepsi to seek minority and women co-packers for diversity and inclusion. I told her about my previous experience with Pepsi and that I needed someone outside the diversity department to help connect me with Pepsi's key decision-maker.

She contacted the head of Pepsi's advisory committee to introduce Hardy Bottling, forwarding our presentation and capability statement. Several months later, I was invited to their New York office to meet the co-pack managers. It was a very good meeting, and they were impressed with both my experience and my facility's capabilities.

Never Put All Your Eggs in One Basket

My second rule of selling is not to put all your eggs in one basket. Pursue multiple prospects with the goal of landing 20 to 50 percent of them. While pursuing Pepsi, Hardy Bottling was also pursuing Coca-Cola. I had used my beverage supplier network to get the right contact at Coke, and that person shared the quality criteria that were important to them. They also shared Coke's capacity concerns. We learned that Coke needed our capabilities and our location was ideal. All we had to do was qualify and pass the third-party audit.

Coke turned out to be a good company for which to provide services. Its co-pack manager was inclusive. She believed in women and minority businesses. She visited Hardy Bottling to tour our facility and meet with both the operations and quality team members. Coke learned firsthand that our team was highly qualified rather than judging them sight unseen.

After the initial visit, Coke performed an audit of the facility and verified our quality testing capabilities. After a successful audit, a product test was scheduled to manufacture the Coke Tab formula. If we were successful, the second test would be to manufacture Coke's energy drink.

After both successful production tests, we were offered a contract with Coca Cola North America (CCNA).

The caveat was that the Coke contract did not allow us to contract with PepsiCo, but they did not restrict business with other beverage companies. Therefore, after signing the Coke contract, we gracefully withdrew from discussions with PepsiCo. I courted Pepsi for over a year and half. In less than six months, we completed Coke's entire process and signed a contract for services. I chose to walk away from Pepsi. I did not know if we would ever get a contract with them, and their leadership was risk-adverse, which could have impacted our future relationship in other ways as well.

Both Pepsi and Coke are great companies. The difference was in the quality of leadership and their willingness to be inclusive and take a risk with a new business. Coke's manager visited

Hardy to gain firsthand information about the team and quality of the facility. Pepsi's leadership chose to judge sight unseen. The value proposition of Hardy was its location, manufacturing capabilities, water, and experienced team. The distribution cost from Memphis was lower than most metropolitan areas based upon its central location. Coke chose to look closely at the financial opportunity while others would not spend the time to even go to first base.

While pursuing business with Pepsi, I followed up at respectful intervals. It is important that you don't make the customer feel you are stalking them for the sake of selling. If a customer tells you they will provide next steps in two weeks, it is okay to follow up after that time has passed. If possible, provide nuggets of new information to them when you do follow up. With Pepsi, I followed up with a copy of our third-party audit designed to communicate the quality of our facility since they did not visit it personally. Next, I sent our water quality report. New information is a valid reason to follow up with a prospect. Conclude each communication by expressing a desire to understand the next steps in their process.

Since I could not sign a contract with both Coke and Pepsi, I eventually had to walk away from Pepsi despite the time I had invested in pursuing business with them. Business owners must know when to walk away from a prospect. In this case, Pepsi's sell cycle had no end in sight and a sure offer was on the table from Coke.

Not All Sales are Good

Many small businesses struggle to grasp the concept that not all customers are good customers. Especially in the beginning, the need for sales tends to overrule common sense. I once had a customer who constantly complained and was always seeking monetary damages. If the order was late, he wanted payment. But if he was late, holding up production, he expected us to understand. If we as a supplier did anything wrong, he wanted the supplies for free. This went on for a few years and the intense scrutiny made the team uneasy, which easily can lead to mistakes. This customer's micromanagement created inefficiencies because my employees would second-guess everything they did.

This is the type of customer you need to walk away from. They are not your partner. They are a good example of an adversary in your house. These are the kinds of customers who do not understand that partners work together for the common good. Eventually, we did not merely walk away from this customer; we ran away. All customers are not good customers.

Overdeliver

Another rule I have for selling is to always overdeliver on what you promise a customer. A bid price or contract proposal includes cost, quality, and service that meets or exceeds the competition's value proposition. Therefore, a new contract award requires the vendor to over deliver as compared to the competition. That pricing must include supplies, overhead, transportation, and any inefficiency caused by the product. The cost of supplies should include supply cost, freight, shrinkage, storage, handling, and your cost of capital. Selling with your heart requires an open mind that is not blinded by the prospect of the sell. A low quote that does not cover the true costs of service requirements could bankrupt the business—and that would tear out your heart.

I always encourage salesmen to underpromise and overdeliver. If a customer needed specialized parts with a typical lead time of five days, they needed to promise that supplier's five-day lead time, no less. However, my team, in an emergency, worked with the supplier to reduce the delivery time to twenty-four hours as the manufacturer's representative. The salesman responsible for that customer relationship personally delivered the parts to the customer's manager. He created goodwill with the key decision-maker, and that salesman's reputation was elevated from dependable to extremely reliable in a crunch. He is now the go-to person for that customer. When the contract was renewed, the customer expanded our services to include some of their other locations. Selling is not always about winning over new customers; sometimes selling is all about loving the one you are with.

Finding New Business

Along with requiring more energy and resources, seeking new customers often requires out-of-the-box thinking. I not only am a member of my local chamber of commerce, but I constantly research industry news. Another example of out-of-the-box thinking could be seeking trade groups in your business sector that host annual trade shows. Trade groups exist for everything from prisons to lumber, grain to chemicals, supplies, logistics, women, minorities, and so many other things. Your state will also have a list of all companies doing business in the state. These are all prospective new customers.

If you desire international customers, you can contact your state export department, the USDA, or a specific country's embassy. For example, when I wanted to secure goods from South America, I called the Portuguese embassy for a contact. When I wanted to sell rice to Mexico, I called the USDA, who provided the USDA contact for Mexico. As you think about your business, make a list of resources for your business. Make a list of trade groups. Develop a list of questions and call them. Ask if they are willing to share last year's trade show information, including the participants' contact information.

Selling with heart ultimately requires you to know sales strengths, your customer, and your competition. Remember that not all customers are good customers. Ideal customers are respectful, trustworthy, and reasonable, and they seek a win-win relationship. Customers who do not value your services, possess unreasonable expectations, or cannot be satisfied are customers to avoid. Most of the information you need to know about potential customers and competitors is just a phone call away. Your suppliers are critical to your network. Suppliers know the customers who use their products and can keep you updated on industry trends. They can provide valuable advice about which trade shows are the best to meet prospects and the requirements of potential customers. The knowledge they provide is critical for being able to sell with your heart and grow your business.

**Based upon your reading about "Sell with Heart,"
what actions will you take? Suggestions:**

Make a list of satisfied customers. Document why you think are they satisfied. Make a list of other services you can offer to your satisfied customers but currently do not.

_____

_____

_____

Make a list of dissatisfied customers and create a brief problem statement for each. List the changes needed and your plans to address those changes. The sales and customer service teams should participate in this exercise.

_____

_____

_____

Write a one-paragraph elevator pitch about your business, including the value proposition.

_____

_____

_____

Make a list of new target companies. How do you compare to each one's current supplier?

_____

_____

_____

Make a list of trade groups and trade shows for networking opportunities.

_____

_____

_____

Chapter 12:

Show Me the Money

business needed to borrow one million dollars to scale up. The owner and managers did not develop a plan for their use of those funds. Instead, they spent the loan on new equipment, new hires, travel, furniture, automobiles, and other items they assumed the business needed. They did not perform a return on investment for each purchase. Twelve months later, the business is out of cash with no increase in sales. The company's credit worthiness declines with accounts payables far exceeding accounts receivables. The company stops paying payroll taxes. Bills are paid late, if at all. As a result, suppliers require prepayment or cash on delivery (COD) for purchases. Customer service suffers and the business loses customers. Finally, the company files for bankruptcy.

This is the story of too many new businesses and 50 percent of small businesses.[8] If you fail to plan, then you plan to fail. A financial plan always includes a use of funds statement. Each planned purchase should have an ROI with key milestones. An accountant would have advised the owner to take a different course of action and potentially prevented the financial fatality.

Financial Planning

When I started Hardy Bottling, I developed a detailed business plan. As part of that, the three-year financial plan included a projected Income Statement, Balance Sheet, and Cash Flow Statement. The plan also included a detailed staffing plan, equipment requirements, inventory, and other spending requirements. Based upon these projections, I developed a plan for the use of funds to guide our actions. The budget included a contingency for missed projections, unexpected expenses, and lagging sales.

The problem with Hardy Bottling's business plan was my conservative projections. As a CPA, my tendency was to underpromise and overdeliver—even to myself. Therefore, the financial projections did not impress banks. The first year's income projected a loss. I planned to borrow working capital that would allow the business to stabilize after two years. The projections showed positive cash flow after year two. My loan request included funding for working capital, equipment overhaul, change parts, inventory, and staffing through year two. I applied for a twenty-five-million-dollar loan. The banks turned me down, but I was eventually approved for a fifteen-million-dollar loan from hard moneylenders at five points above prime, enough to get us started.

That financial plan was my business guide. I updated it frequently as business circumstances changed. Managers making unplanned spending requests had to justify the cost, and they learned to analyze each request. Will the expenditure increase sales? If so, how much? They learned to be specific as well, since "a lot" is not a measurable number. Will the expenditure reduce costs? If so, how much?

For example, at Hardy, our highest utility bill was 387,000.00 dollars per month for electricity. This was the number one threat to our survival. Smaller air compressors were recommended, but they were not in the budget. However, one vendor offered to install units at no cost to test for a few months, and the units were successful in saving us over 50,000 dollars per month. The electric utility cost reductions paid for the units in less than three months.

Most business owners are not accountants, nor do they have accounting experience. Most hated accounting in school. An accountant is as important as any business specialist. An accountant can allow the owner to focus on business growth while the accountant focuses on the financial well-being of the company.

After a financial plan is developed with spending rules, accountants can also ensure that management adheres to the plan. They track sales, spending, and cash flow and compare them to the plan. They make sure customers are invoiced, funds are received, and taxes are paid. Accountants sweat the details, such as daily monitoring of cash to minimize surprises. They can provide a projection of when you're going to be out of cash as opposed to the typical model of a business realizing they are out of cash when the bank account is overdrawn. There are few actions available at the last minute to cover this shortfall unless you have a line of credit. Therefore, an accountant's services can eliminate these surprises as the eyes and ears of the business's financial health.

By far, the hardest position to retain at my company was the accountant. Accountants are in high demand since small businesses compete for talent with Fortune 500 companies. A small business needs talent with broader skills than Fortune 500 companies because a small business accountant has a wider range of responsibility. My accountants quit because their scope of responsibilities was too broad, took too many hours, and came with fewer benefits. Thankfully, during vacancies in the accounting role, I was able to fill the void since I started my career as a CPA. This was not my favorite contribution to my business, but it was a necessary use of my skills and training.

Finding an Accountant

For those who do not have CPA training in their background, there are several ways to fill an accounting vacancy that may pan out better than the traditional search for talent. At times, I hired an accountant through Accountemps, a temporary agency that specializes in placing accounting professionals. This provided a temporary solution until a full-time replacement was hired. I also used Accountemps to evaluate potential hires and ensure the candidate was a good fit before offering a permanent position. This allowed us to try before we buy, which minimized the impact on the morale of permanent employees when temporary employees were not a good fit and had to be reassigned.

Establishing a relationship with the local CPA society can also identify professionals seeking side jobs. I was a member of the local American Women's Society of Certified Public Accountants. Some CPA professionals work part-time outside their full-time employment hours. Sometimes a company will hire a full-time accounting clerk to handle day-to-day transactions and the part-time CPA would establish policies, prepare and review reports, provide advice to management, and ensure adherence to policy. The part-time CPA would also monitor cash flow, prepare monthly financials, and develop ROIs for capital requests. They can be a valuable financial advisor to the CEO.

Another great option for finding an accountant is a service such as Meritan, a great source of retired professionals. I hired an accountant who had retired from a local automotive plant. He had started a search for employment only six months after retiring. He missed his profession and the daily interaction. Most retirees need a lot of time off and shorter workdays. Otherwise, they are just grateful to continue working. They can be extremely loyal and reliable and typically have a broader range of experience than most accountants.

You might also consider sharing a full-time accountant with another company. This typically gives you access to an accountant five days a week. The two companies agree on the number of days each one may require, and the accountant can focus on two small businesses, which can be efficient and effective.

Financial Management

Lack of financial management ranks as one of the top five reasons new and small businesses fail. Controlling your business requires managing incoming and outgoing cash. A lack of financial management results in a company flying blindly, but this is realistically a pretty normal mode of operation for small businesses. Why? Small businesses treat the business cash management with the same afterthought as their personal finances: Money is not a problem—until it is.

Some small businesses have the misconception that an outside accounting firm is only qualified to do taxes, but an accountant's job includes managing the financial health of the company. Financials is the monthly wellness check for the business, and accountants are like the doctor. They can advise the business owner in advance of a cash fatality. Regardless of their own knowledge and skill when it comes to money, a business owner is responsible for the financial well-being of the business; ignorance is not an excuse, especially when that ignorance can be solved with the help of an accountant.

A second financial reason that businesses fail is insufficient working capital to weather the highs and lows of the business. If nothing else, the last recession demonstrated that business is cyclical. A business will encounter bad times and good times due to both controllable and non-controllable events. The gain or loss of an important customer or critical employee, the arrival of a new competitor, or the filing of a lawsuit can cause fluctuations. Most businesses do not survive business downturns because they are unprepared for those fluctuations. And if a company is out of cash with no borrowing capacity, they may not survive.

At one point, Hardy Bottling wanted to expand our services to existing customers. A new case packer was required to offer services to pack four- and six-pack cans. Either I was leaving profits on the table or my customers were using other packers for this service, but we could not afford to purchase this machine. I told the equipment vendor that I needed the machine but could not purchase it and asked if we could come up with a creative solution. We negotiated a lease arrangement that allowed me to secure the machine without stressing our working capital.

> *As my daughter says, a closed mouth does not get fed.*

Sometimes you have to put pride aside, open your mouth, and ask the question; people cannot read your mind. Asking for a lease or seeking creative payment options will not kill you. The worst someone can say is "no."

The goal is always to secure the equipment you need without stressing working capital. An accountant will process loan paperwork and evaluate loan options for you. The most frequently used financial options include:

- A **capital lease** is a lease in which the leaser only finances the leased asset, and all other rights of ownership transfer to the lessee. The asset is recorded as the lessee's property in its general ledger as a fixed asset. The cost of the asset is recorded as a liability. This rate, typically the cost plus the interest, is allocated over the term of the lease.

- An **operating lease** is a contract that allows the use of an asset but does not convey rights of ownership of the asset. The lease payment can be significantly lower since you do not own the asset.

- A **bank loan** for the asset uses the asset as collateral. Also, the business must be bankable and demonstrate its ability to service the debt.

- A **bank line of credit** typically requires a guarantor since no asset is available as collateral. Also, the business must be bankable and demonstrate its ability to service the debt.

- A **business accelerator program** gives companies access to mentorship, investors, and other support that helps them become stable, self-sufficient businesses. Companies that use business accelerators are typically startups that have moved beyond the earliest stages of getting established. They may offer loans ranging from 10,000 to 100,000 dollars.

- **Venture capital funds** are investment companies that manage the money of investors who seek private equity stakes in startup and small- to medium-sized enterprises with strong growth potential. These investments are generally characterized as high-risk/high-return opportunities.

- Never use credit card debt to purchase equipment unless you plan to pay in full. There are typically high interest rates and fees. Also, high credit card debt has a negative impact on your credit rating and the business credit worthiness.

Your accountant, CPA firm, and/or lawyer should review financing proposals' interest rates, fees, penalties, assignment, prepayment penalties, etc. I have seen contracts with fees as high as the interest rate that will get you in trouble down the line if you are not careful.

Most businesses operate on a small amount of cash with accounts receivables equaling accounts payables. A healthy company needs cash to cover the cyclical nature of business. Most companies depend upon the timely payment of accounts receivables to meet accounts payables obligations. Accounts receivables net thirty-day timing is too late to meet accounts payables, net thirty-day or the weekly payroll. For example, let's say at the end of the month, receivables equal 100,000 dollars, while payables equal 90,000 dollars. If receivables are always received before payables are due, you have no problem. But in the real world, customers are slow to pay receivables and vendors charge a late fee for payables after thirty days. A business should always have 25 to 50 percent of the payables expenses as working capital or have a line of credit to handle timing issues. This mismatched timing can cause late payments, negatively impacting credit ratings.

Having an accountant handle monthly financials can also help identify high- and low-earning months so you can develop a cash flow plan. A simple rule for estimating your cash needs is to divide annual sales by twelve. Multiply the results by 50 percent. So, if your sales are twelve million dollars, you need a minimum of 500,000 dollars in cash. This formula ensures timely bill payment and cash reserves for inventory, operations, and emergencies.

Excess Profit

Although excess profit may not seem like something that requires planning, even that excess should be managed with care. How should your company use those excess profits? I'll give you a hint: It's not by spending them on a new car or the vacation you've always wanted. For that excess profit, your options include strengthening your cash position and cash reserves, paying down high-interest debt, such as credit cards or loans, investing in growing your business, or making a lump sum payment on your line of credit. You can draw down the line of credit in the future, if necessary. Also, consider giving employees a bonus to let them know you appreciate them.

A small note on payroll: It is reported that the number one mistake for businesses is failure to make timely payroll tax deposits.[9] Some companies establish a separate payroll bank account to manage payroll. Many companies' accountants file payroll taxes and quarterly tax reports. Personally, I hired a payroll service to process employee payroll, make federal tax deposits, and file reports. I use payroll services for all my companies since those services are typically low-cost and efficient. The best option for small businesses is to hire a payroll service.

In closing, sound financial management is key to the success—and the survival—of your business. Successful companies require top professionals like accountants to lead financial planning and management, allowing the CEO or owner to focus on growing the business. Companies need sufficient working capital to manage and grow the business. The challenge is finding the right amount of working capital, and an accountant can help find that answer while managing cash flow. An accountant's role is managing the financial health of the business. If the pulse of the business is high or low, they make recommendations to help get it back on track. Managing your business without an accountant is as dangerous as flying a plane without instruments. Do you want to guide your business to a planned landing or fly out of control until you run out of fuel? Regular financial checkups to "show you the money" will ensure you land safely.

Based upon your reading about "Show Me the Money," what actions will you take? Suggestions:

What is your credit score? If it's bad, order a complete copy of your credit report. Are you paying your bills on time? If not, why not?

_____

_____

_____

Make a list of debts, including: type of debt, balance due, term, interest rate, and monthly payment.

_____

_____

_____

Divide your annual sales by twelve then multiply that by 50 percent. This is the ideal amount of cash your business should have on hand. The minimum is 25 percent of accounts payable. How much cash do you have on hand? Make a list of options to handle a working capital shortfall.

_____

_____

_____

Ask a CPA firm to analyze your financial statements. A CPA firm will typically perform this analysis at no cost to you as a new prospect.

_____

_____

_____

Chapter 13:

Growing Pains

Evan Singer, General Manager of SmartBiz, said it best, "If there's anything we know about small businesses, it's that they are always focused on growth. Small businesses are investing in the future by buying new equipment and real estate, hiring new employees, and increasing inventory, as well as refinancing debt to get lower payments."

Businesses across the country struggle to grow each year. New contracts are wonderful, but they normally require more cash, new equipment, additional staffing, or increased inventory. The reality is that with limited working capital, access to top talent, and ability to obtain a bank loan, small business growth is restricted. These companies often desperately seek creative options to grow their business.

Be Careful How You Grow

The mission of Hardy Bottling was to offer a full line of packaging services to beverage brands across the United States at competitive prices. At one point, Hardy had eight packaging lines but could not afford to purchase change parts. A change part is a tool that allows the same equipment to run different packaging sizes. The cost of a change part was less than 5 percent of the full equipment cost, but we were struggling to find creative options to fund our growth. Hardy's working capital challenge was similar to most businesses: We had enough funds to operate but not enough to grow.

At the same time as we were trying to find creative options to fund change parts, the COO of FRS approached me to produce their fast-growing new energy drink. The current FRS spokesperson was Lance Armstrong, who had won two consecutive Tour de France bike races. The energy drink was unique in using quercetin rather than caffeine as its key active ingredient. FRS positioned its product as all-natural and healthier than other energy drinks. They claimed the body did not experience the typical crash associated with most energy drinks.

The only problem was that the FRS product was in a twelve-ounce slim can. Hardy Bottling could produce every can type except this one. The FRS opportunity would generate a minimum of three million dollars in annual revenue. Additionally, there were five other beverage prospects that needed this same can that we were currently leaving on the table. This was the fastest-growing beverage package in the industry. In order to grow and thrive, we needed this capability and the contract with FRS.

The cost to convert one of our four can packaging lines was over 300,000 dollars. We lacked the capital for the conversion, and the equipment vendor required a 50 percent down payment with the balance due upon completion of the conversion. We met with banks for financing, but the loan was denied because this was a machine modification, not new equipment, and we had weak financials the prior year. We were desperate for a creative solution.

FRS said they would pay for the conversion, but their condition was that the line would be limited to FRS products. Businesses must be careful to avoid desperate deals that result in one-sided contracts, such as the one FRS proposed. I wanted the opportunity, but their terms would limit my ability to use a five-million-dollar packaging line for other customers. I was desperate, not crazy.

So, I started thinking about who else would benefit from our additional twelve-ounce slim can capacity and who possessed the ability to loan us funds. We made a list of companies who met the criteria. The first name on the list was FRS. They could use 50 percent of our capacity, but I already knew their terms. The other companies on the list were too small to pay for a conversion. The list included both large carton and can companies. I moved on to a list of relationships that might benefit from and fund this request. My first contact was my customer relations manager at Ball Corporation, a company that produces cans and ends for beverages. The value proposition presented to Ball was that Hardy would dedicate an entire packaging line to this package type. This would increase Ball's capacity by 500 million cans for this high-demand package. She reviewed the request with her president, and, after a few weeks, I had a deal. The payment required me to sell a set number of can ends to new customers for Ball, and I was only required to pay the shortfall. This was a great deal—a much more agreeable cost for growth than the deal proposed by FRS.

Within three months, the line conversion was complete. I immediately signed the smaller customers. Within a year, I also started producing for FRS. This increase in sales generated excess funds to finance further growth. This ended up being a smart move that improved our relationship with Ball Corporation and did not cost us the business with FRS. Ball Corporation even started referring new customers to Hardy Bottling to take advantage of our new capacity, which grew sales for both companies.

Understanding the Cost of Growth

I always advise business owners to make sure they understand the cost of new contracts. The cost of a contract includes equipment as well as additional human capital and working capital. When we expanded to the twelve-ounce slim can, the cost was 300,000 dollars plus five additional employees. So I needed 300,000 dollars and five people to gain over three million dollars in new revenue. This growth did not require a monthly payment since the deal involved growing the vendor's business as well.

It took guts to ask for money and say, "I can grow your business." But it was true, and it works. This was a true win-win.

An example of growth that was not such a win-win was a business that went bankrupt after winning a new contract for janitorial services. The company's largest contract produced 300,000 dollars annually. Its service quality was exceptional and priced competitively. Initially, the company serviced 25 percent of a specific corporation's janitorial contract. The next year, they were awarded 100 percent of the contract.

The problem was that the payment terms were net sixty days.

The janitorial company applied for a line of credit to support the expansion. Banks denied the loan because the company's financials from the prior year showed that its cash flow would not service the debt. The banks would not even consider the new contract. Without the line of credit, the janitorial company could not staff at the required level for the new contract. Additionally, the company was paying its new employees late, resulting in high turnover.

The staff worked overtime to service the new contract. Service and quality suffered. Within a year, the business lost both its reputation and largest customer. Growth destroyed this company because of its inability to expand its working capital. Many business bankruptcies have a similar story: They go bankrupt by signing a new contract before having enough working capital.

Most businesses understand the cost of growth. Janitorial companies typically staff by square footage. Service companies staff technicians based upon estimated service calls. The problem is not a lack of knowledge but a lack of access to capital that leads to desperate decisions.

Higher sales can help finance growth, but favorable payment terms are required for this to be effective. In my businesses, when large customer accounts receivables were late, placing the business at risk of being late with our account payables, I contacted the customer. I always contacted the larger customers myself. Typically, they operate on a line of credit and could afford payment. My go-to company for my first call was Rockstar, who always accommodated my request. In addition, we had some prepaid customers who paid two weeks in advance. These terms gave prepaid customers first priority on scheduling. In this case, it was their cash, rather than size, that got them to the head of the line and helped us avoid being late with our account payables.

Ask

The janitorial service that went bankrupt could have worked preventatively and negotiated fifteen-day payment terms for the first year. In most cases, the corporation would have granted those terms, understanding the growing pains small businesses face. The problem is that most small businesses will not ask.

Growth requires small businesses to compete on cost, quality, and service. When I resumed brewing, I needed to purchase small quantities of brewing ingredients to test the system, which were extremely expensive. So, I contacted Anheuser-Busch for a favor. As a larger company, they have large procurement contracts for all brewing ingredients. I shared my dilemma and asked them to leverage their buying power for my business.

Why would they help me? As a small company, they did not view me as a competitor, and they wanted to help smaller companies. I needed brewing ingredients to test the brewery startup. Anheuser-Busch told its suppliers to assist me at their contract price. And my problem was solved. It can never hurt to swallow your pride and just ask. The worst they can say is "no."

> *The longer you are in business, the more you realize the real failure is not asking.*

When you do ask for a favor or a change in terms, the duration of the special payment terms should be minimum one year but not the length of the contract. Explain to your customer that the short-term exception gives your business time to expand its line of credit. In most cases, major corporations understand the plight of small businesses.

I would also advise you to avoid factoring as an option. Factoring typically charges a minimum of 5 percent interest for thirty days. This rate typically consumes all profits of a company. If this approach is necessary, I recommend a community bank if you sell receivables from major customers. Community banks understand that major customers are credit worthy; therefore, they will charge much lower interest rates.

You can also consider expanding your business without permanent staffing by using a temporary agency to provide the additional staffing you need for a new contract. The ideal temporary agency will accept payment terms that match your contract. Larger temporary agencies have more working capital flexibility than smaller one. You can even negotiate the right to hire employees after one year without a placement fee.

The last option for easing growing pains is subcontracting services to a competitor. Your company remains the prime contractor. Your company controls the quality of service and point of contact. Then, as your financials become stronger, you can grow into servicing the contract.

Easing growing pains requires out-of-the-box thinking, bold actions, and willingness to seek non-traditional solutions. There are no crazy questions or requests when looking for ways to grow your business. Analyze each option to ensure the deal benefits you, solves your problem, and does not limit growth. Companies will work with you, but you must be bold enough to ask. In all cases, avoid giving up control. Whatever options you choose, always protect your reputation. Typically, a new contract will cause growing pains, but flexibility with working and human capital ensures that growth does not kill your business.

Based upon your reading about "Growing Pains," what actions will you take? Suggestions:

Assess your company's readiness for a big contract: capacity, human capital, and working capital.

_____

_____

_____

Meet with a banker to discuss financing options, i.e., a line of credit or loan to support growth. List their qualification requirements.

_____

_____

_____

List creative growth options, such as outsourcing or additional automation to increase capacity.

_____

_____

_____

List unprofitable contracts you can prune to create capacity.

_____

_____

_____

What has been holding back the growth of your current services
or your ability offer new services?

_____

_____

_____

Chapter 14:

Speak Up

Mark Sanborn is an author, professional speaker, and entrepreneur best known for his book *The Fred Factor: How Passion in Your Work and Life Can Turn the Ordinary into the Extraordinary.* In it, he says, "In teamwork, silence isn't golden, it's deadly." For a team to function effectively, there must be open channels of communication. When team members don't feel like they can voice concerns, express disagreement, or offer suggestions, it's a sign that there's something chronically wrong with the team. A business owner's job is to make sure everybody on their team knows that dialogue is always welcome.

When Less is More

While dialogue should always be welcome, as a staff accountant, I had a tendency to share too much information. I wanted everyone to understand; therefore, I provided too many details. One time, I was appointed as tour guide for Smucker's board of directors, which included Bill Wrigley. My mentor and I rehearsed the entire schedule to control timing. I was told to stay on script and on schedule.

During the tour, while explaining the operation, we encountered a commotion. Employees were feverishly pulling product off the conveyor while allowing other product to pass. A board member asked what was going on. My inclination was to provide a thorough response, which would have been off script. The plant manager was monitoring my comments on the radio. As soon as the question was asked, he held his breath on the other end of the radio. He knew my typical response was to give a detailed explanation. Instead, I stayed on script and praised employees for doing their job. I told them employees were removing product from the line for inspection at the supervisor's request and moved to the next phase of the tour. In reality, employees had spotted misapplied labels that needed to be placed on quality hold, but that would have been more detailed information than was necessary for this tour. The plant manager complimented how I handled this unexpected situation.

As I explained in a previous chapter, my mentor taught me to practice the three Bs of communication. When providing a response, a speaker should: Be Brief, Be Bright, and Be Gone. Less is usually more when providing a response to your customer. A lengthy response tends to just create more questions or uncertainty. The three Bs means answering the question without adding a lot of extra information. I have observed salesman get the sale but then lose the sale because they kept talking. Encourage your team members to share their ideas but be passionate about the position without rambling. The problem with rambling is that whoever is listening soon forgets the important points. You must speak up to be heard, but you also must stick to the topic and minimize off-topic small talk to be heard. Stay on point.

Speak Up

During their product trial at Hardy Bottling, Coke sent five quality technicians and the co-pack manager to observe the qualification run. Whenever Coke was on-site, my team's stress levels were elevated. Coke's five technicians were giving Hardy's two technicians orders to perform tests that were not on the test plan. As a result, Hardy's technicians could not perform the plan's original required tests. They had to be comfortable speaking up in order to save the test plan.

The VP of operations notified me that Coke's technicians were causing a disruption, and Coke's co-pack manager was sent to my office. I explained that her quality technicians were overwhelming Hardy's. My technicians were not able to adhere to the test plan because of the extra activities. I gave her two options: We could either modify the test plan or remove the extra activities. I wanted Coke to have what they needed; therefore, we agreed that Coke's technicians would perform the extra activities.

The employees' willingness to speak up saved the plant's performance on Coke's test. They were able to perform the test plan required by Coke while Coke's technicians performed extra activities not outlined in the test plan. Our message was: We are on your team; we will perform the test plan and do everything possible to deliver extra services. Based on this experience, we scheduled extra personnel to support tests for customers moving forward.

The Right Person

In business, it is critical to not just communicate but communicate to the right person. Speaking up to the wrong person can be viewed as gossip. The first person to deliver a concern or opportunity to the key decision-maker is labeled a valuable team player that demonstrates concerns for the business. The decision-maker characterizes the messenger as thoughtful, creative, and mature. Sharing concerns or gossip around the office before discussing with management will change management's view of the communication. By waiting to share the concern with the right person, the concern might devalue you or label you as a gossiping troublemaker. It's not what you say but how and when you say it. I immediately communicated directly with Coke's co-pack manager that we would follow the agreed-upon test plan. We made our best efforts to provide additional services. We showed we were on their team. In the end, Coke praised us for doing a great job, and they also praised our employees for speaking up and adhering to the test plan.

Delivery

There are times when a business owner must take charge. I tell other business owners that the good days are gifts; the CEO and managers are paid for the bad days. The type of communication I had with Coke is critical to the success of your business. You can constructively say "no" to additional requests while affirming your commitment to the customer. Additionally, this type of communication should happen in private with sensitivity. My communication with Coke could have resulted in them demanding more support, which would have required negotiations. But addressing it at the right place and the right time allowed all parties to save face and achieve the desired outcome.

Sometimes who delivers the message is just as important as the message itself. I will never forget running a test batch for a major craft brewer. The test was well-planned. We were confident our brewing system and water would deliver a superior product, which could lead to a major contract with a craft brewer. We brewed the product, completed fermentation ... and the batch went down the sewer system! The VP of operations came to my office in shock. After she told me about the loss, I was in shock as well. I pulled myself together to get details about what happened and asked if we saved any of the test products. But it was all lost, and I had to be the one to let the customer know.

During the meeting with the customer, I first thanked the customer for performing the test. I also stated that we were happy to share the cost of this test. We had contributed our co-pack services at no charge, and the craft brewer contributed the ingredients. I then shared the news that the batch was lost due to a valve malfunction. I asked if the customer had tasted and tested the product at each step since the end batch was lost. Thankfully, he had, and he was satisfied with the results. I apologized for the lost batch and explained that this type of problem can happen during startup. We offered to repeat the test, but the customer did not feel it was necessary. He appreciated our communication, stated the mission was accomplished— and we passed.

Open Communication

Author Elizabeth W. Morrison from the Stern School of Business at New York University believes employee silence is a real problem. In her article "Employee Voice and Silence," Morrison defines "voice" in the workplace as informal communication from an employee to someone higher up in the organizational hierarchy and warns: "If voice is withheld within an organizational context, both performance and employee morale may suffer, so the consequences may be significant. In addition, there is evidence suggesting that voice is in fact stifled in many organizations and that employees are often very hesitant to engage in voice, particularly when the information could be viewed by the recipient as negative or threatening."[10]

Employees voicing concerns, such as Coke's technicians not adhering to the test plan, was critical to our success with that contract. If employees had adhered to Coke's additional requests rather than the test plan, Hardy would have failed. Your business's success is dependent upon employees speaking their minds about the company's operations or policies. Employees should not fear reprimand or punishment. Hardy Bottling's team had embraced Smucker's quality system of "Quality at the Source." It was our company culture for each individual to own the quality of product and customer care. The success of this test from Coke demonstrated the value of employees' voices.

The best way to create an environment of open communication is by helping leadership understand that employees are not robots. Feeling like what they see, think, and feel are valued causes employees to voice their opinions. These attributes are what make human collateral so valuable.

Why would an employee put his job (or business) on the line to save your business if they are not heard? The job must become the employee's business. It is how he or she makes a living. Therefore, management must communicate through their actions that employees' opinions and sharing of information is not subject to retaliation.

For example, an employee observing a manager breaking a safety policy or engaging in troubling behavior would not be the victim of retaliation in my businesses. This employee's voice could save a life or a contract by making their company aware of the situation.

Management must understand that "Quality at the Source" is only effective if employees are empowered to speak up. "Quality at the Source" requires employees to own product quality at their stage of production. Each employee's decisions and opinions matter and their input is expected and appreciated. Engaged employees freely share what's on their minds. My employees were customer-focused and understood the importance of adherence to specifications. They had the authority to stop production and speak with management about production specifications and customer requests whenever they had a concern. Leadership valuing employees' opinions gave everyone a sense of pride and responsibility.

How can businesses create a competitive advantage in today's world of e-commerce and social media? The competition is always selling the same service or widget, earning the same margins, with a similar supply chain. Customers are looking for different value propositions that add to the bottom line. Employees' inclusion in developing the new value proposition is critical for the future. Customers expect businesses to solve real-time problems, which is dependent upon individual employees with the knowledge, authority, and confidence to act. Employees who are loyal to their company can deliver this exceptional service, which is itself a huge value proposition. They are your first line of defense when connecting to customers. A workforce that is encouraged and expected to speak up with an effective voice is the secret weapon that differentiates your company from the competition. Remember, everyone wants to be heard, and I can guarantee you someone is listening.

Based upon your reading about "Speak Up," what actions will you take? Suggestions:

Make a list of recent employee ideas. If you have to think too long, you may have a problem that you need to address. It could demonstrate that employees are not comfortable being open with you.

_____

_____

_____

Make a list of employees who tend to share news—both good and bad.

_____

_____

_____

Do employees have authority to act? Are they asking you permission for every decision? Do they ask for guidance on simple decisions? Ask them to make a decision, and then support their decision.

_____

_____

_____

How are you encouraging employees to share ideas or opinions with management?

_____

_____

_____

Chapter 15:

Provide Equipment

Chandra Steele wrote in her article titled "Outdated Technology in the Workplace Costs Companies" that ZenBusiness surveyed 917 office workers about the state of technology in their workplaces. The survey showed that businesses have a serious issue with having outdated computers, printers, software, and other technology.[11] Employers are reluctant to upgrade because of the cost, but they miss the costs of employee morale and productivity.

This technology challenge spans all job levels and departmental functions, and it impacts a business's effectiveness and efficiency. What can your business do to overcome this obstacle? What can you as a manager or business leader do to proactively use this challenge as an opportunity to make a significant cultural improvement in your organization?

A difference in perspective between management and employees is the primary reason resource requests are denied. Management believes the tools are good enough; therefore, employee concerns are minimized. Employees must learn to work around the problem the best they can. The result is workplace frustration, poor morale, reduced productivity, and declining financial performance. The first step is for management to understand that providing the right tools and equipment is part of their job and it is a necessary part of business growth as well.

For example, Industrial Sales, a maintenance repair and operating supply distributor, had a phone system that would fail during every heavy rain. The system would be down for a day or two. Employees said the problem had occurred for many years before I acquired the company. After the first incident, I contacted the phone service provider. They said we needed to upgrade to fiber cabling, so I received quotes from Comcast, AT&T, and WorldSpice. The previous owner said it would be too expensive, but AT&T was approximately 40 percent lower than other service providers. The phone system also had to be replaced since it was not compatible with the new cable. This increased our monthly telephone bill but improved our reliability, morale, and internet speeds. The ROI was immediate by demonstrating that providing the right tools for both customers and employees was important to the company.

It can be expensive, but management must provide the right equipment to maximize employees' performance. There is an old saying that goes: "You are only as good as the tools you use." This saying emphasizes that there is a right tool for every job. As a result, employees are only as efficient or effective as the tools they are provided. At Industrial Sales, we subsequently replaced the computer server and office furniture. The computer server increased efficiency and was necessary to support newer technology. The new furniture supported the company's image and expectations and sent the message that Industrial Sales would compete at a higher level. It also made employees proud of their workplace.

Some examples of tools include human resource systems, computers, devices, warehouse equipment, telephones, software applications, forklifts, pallet jacks, or anything else needed to perform a job. There are thousands of tools with costs ranging from very cheap to incredibly expensive.

Finding the Right Tools

So how do you find the right tools? The most reliable person to ask about what the right tool is would be an employee. Business success requires providing the right tools to employees to do their work effectively. The job is more complicated without the right equipment. Providing the right equipment allows employees to expand their capabilities and capacity, and no one knows what that is better than the person doing the job every day. With Industrial Sales, it was an employee who came to me to discuss his frustrations with the phone system's continued failure. Based upon their concern, it was my first problem solved. The right equipment is the backbone of most business processes.

Business owners must realize that the right equipment creates competitive advantages in cost, quality, and service. If employees aren't provided with the correct tools, they will have to use whatever is available. This can lead to inefficient, slow work, resulting in higher cost, poor quality, and poor service. Your business is only as good as its tools.

I started with the Smucker Company as a staff accountant. When I started, the office manager refused to assign me a telephone even though all administrative employees were assigned a telephone. The office manager was using her authority to purchase equipment as power over me. (This was the downside of having a small-minded and insecure person as a boss.) As a young professional, I vowed to always make sure my team members had the right equipment to perform their jobs and never to use my authority inappropriately.

When I moved into my role as quality manager, my job was to implement quality programs, which included training and providing the necessary tools. Training was designed to enhance the skill sets of the workforce. World-class quality programs train operators to understand all specifications and testing in order to optimize first-time quality. We believed in "Quality at the Source," meaning operators are the best first line of defense to avoid and/or minimize quality problems—but they are only as good as their training and tools. After training all employees, quality technicians continued to work with operators to enhance the training's effectiveness.

After developing new quality manuals and training, "Quality at the Source" was implemented. The operators were responsive to our new techniques for delivering first-time quality, which minimized waste and having to redo work. Operators were trained to perform new testing procedures to validate product quality at each station before packaging, and quality technicians assisted operators for weeks by observing how they performed the new techniques and providing timely feedback.

An example of the right tools being essential can be found in the story of a label operator who was struggling with the new technique to measure front and back label placement. The gauge was a straight metal ruler. It had to be placed perfectly to accurately perform the test. The quality technician recommended disqualifying this label operator from her job. This would have reduced her wage, forced her into another job, and maybe forced her into another shift. She would also lose confidence in herself. This label operator was dependable, consistent, supportive, and a team player. She was the type of employee all companies want—and need—with character traits that cannot be trained.

Management felt the struggle was the label operator's problem and failure. But I felt the company had failed this employee by not providing training that met her needs. The price of progress is not cheap, and employees are really the ones who pay the price of change. I challenged management to find a better solution than disqualifying her. They found an L-shaped ruler that could be positioned in the same place each time, eliminating the struggle to place it exactly every time. This solved the problem, which saved a valuable employee. The equipment cost was less than ten dollars. This demonstrated to all employees, not just the label operator, that the company would go the extra mile for them. I challenge every business owner to invest in the right tools rather than risk destroying an employee's life.

Companies that provide the right equipment allow employees to perform their jobs effectively and efficiently. When considering new equipment, companies often focus on the equipment cost without considering the labor cost.

For example, the time it takes to unload a truck of grain meal ranges from thirty minutes to an hour and a half. The difference is that efficient drivers use a vibrator, while other drivers use a rubber hammer to physically hit the truck. As you evaluate your employees' equipment, ask: Do they have what they need to do the job? There was a grain company that was losing two deliveries a day for lack of proper equipment when the payback on the equipment was less than five days. And the impact on employee satisfaction? Priceless.

Safety

Safety cost can be a confusing topic, but the bottom line is that the right tools can reduce accidents and worker compensation insurance premiums. Employees' perception of excessive accidents is that they are just taking money from the insurance company, but in actuality, each company's experience rating is used to calculate its premiums. At Coors, we calculated worker's compensation cost per case since our employees understood this metric. Our cost was five to ten times higher than other breweries, so our safety program was low-hanging fruit to reduce cost. In addition, our poor safety rating had a negative impact on employee morale. Employees are always your best source when it comes to selecting the right equipment. Ask employees to provide recommendations for personal protective equipment to improve safety. Analyze safety logs and reports for types of accidents and each one's frequency. Procuring equipment to improve safety communicates to employees that the company cares about them, while reducing costs at the same time.

After implementing the requests for equipment or tools, give the credit for the change to employees. This shows the staff you are listening and responsive, and buy-in from employees predicts a positive outcome. If a specific change is too expensive, explain why. Ask employees to recommend less expensive alternatives. Employees manage households every day. They are accustomed to weighing alternatives if you give them the opportunity.

The smallest and largest investments in business are the needs of employees. Investing in tools employees need to do their jobs sends many positive messages. Responding to an employee's request for a tool to make their job more efficient tells that employee you care about their voice and the business. If you don't respond, the perception of employees is that you don't care. The right tools can change the attitude of employees, which impacts efficiency and company loyalty. How would military and police personnel feel without the right tools each day in situations where lives are at stake? What messages was Industrial Sales sending to employees and customers each time the phone system was down for days? The new message is: We value you and your services. The right equipment for employees is simple the cost of doing good business.

Based upon your reading about "Provide Equipment," what actions will you take? Suggestions:

Make a list of complaints from employees that are still open. Do they need a better telephone system, faster computer, bigger monitors, chairs, coffee maker, etc.?

_____

_____

_____

List the tools that were purchased in the last twelve months.

_____

_____

_____

Meet with employees to discuss tools they need to improve safety. Review your accident log.

_____

_____

_____

Have exit interviews with employees who resign to understand whether equipment impacted their decision to leave.

_____

_____

_____

Chapter 16:

Signing on the Dotted Line

One time, a company asked Hardy Bottling if they could use the brewery to produce biofuel. They lacked the funding for the capital investment and the working capital to convert and operate the brewery as a biofuel facility. After we toured the facility and discussed the feasibility of their project, we decided it was not the best use of our assets. We never entered into an agreement.

A few weeks later, I received a call from a friend telling me that the group had posted pictures of my brewery on their website. The website stated that my facility was their asset. I asked my lawyer to send a cease and desist letter stating we would sue them for damages if they refused to comply. The pictures were removed, and I never heard from them again. There was no agreement with them—written or oral. The letter from my lawyer ensured they were clear on my intent. I was able to walk away because I did not sign on the dotted line.

Avoiding Bad Deals

One dotted line small businesses should avoid is making desperate deals with equity investors. Equity investors invest money into a company in exchange for a share of ownership. Equity investors have no guarantee of a return on their investment, and they may lose their money should the company go bankrupt. If the business is contemplating an equity deal in exchange for services, first get quotes for the retail value of the bartered service. For example, a lawyer offered his services handling Hardy Bottling's purchase agreement in exchange for 5 percent of the company. I asked him to send me a quote for his legal services.

The first red flag was his hesitancy to provide a quote. He then communicated that the average cost was 150,000 dollars. Meanwhile, I was acquiring an asset valued at forty million dollars. He wanted 5 percent, which was valued at two million dollars, for 150,000 dollars in services. The gentleman was a predator as well as an insult to my intelligence. If I decided to use his services, I would pay in cash.

Of course, I do not use predatory services. This was a when-hell-freezes-over moment.

The lesson here is to tread lightly when forming agreements during desperate times with predators, family, and friends. A lawyer (a non-predatory one) can provide unemotional objectivity. This is necessary since you as the business owner may be emotional. Agreements inked in the early years of a business often become a problem when the business achieves an unexpected level of success.

Early in the business life cycle, agreements are typically homegrown, i.e., not written by an attorney. The perception of businesses in the early stages is they are not worth much. There is little thought given to future valuations. Therefore, provisions such as voting rights, rights to sell, conflict of interest, etc., are missed. New businesses always need cash, customer contracts, or services, but how desperate are you? Will you agree to anything to save your company or idea? The decisions you make today can—and will—haunt you tomorrow.

When I was an accountant with Smucker's, I made the mistake of not reading the fine print on the Xerox lease agreement, which turned out to have an automatic renewal provision. Smucker's was required to send a written cancellation letter ninety days prior to the expiration date. We missed the cancellation terms, and the lease automatically renewed even though we had already leased a smaller, faster color copier. This mistake cost us another year's lease. And I faced this mistake every day for twelve long months. The Xerox copier sitting in the hallway was a constant reminder of the cost of not reading and complying with a contract in full. It was a costly lesson, but one I will never forget.

When Hardy Bottling needed to purchase three shrink-wrap machines to expand contract packaging services, it looked like the cost of the machines would deplete 100 percent of the company's working capital. I met with several banks to secure an equipment loan, and they reviewed our financials to evaluate our ability to service the debt. The financials showed that our cash flow was not enough to service the new debt.

Our second option was to secure an equipment lease from the equipment manufacturer, but the manufacturer did not offer a lease option.

The last option was to find a company that sold supplies as a condition to lease the equipment. A division of International Paper, xpedx, was my shrink-wrap supplier when I was a VP for Coors, and they offered to purchase the three machines. They sold cartons, paper, and other packaging supplies that Hardy Bottling customers used. They offered Hardy a lease purchase agreement in exchange for the machines.

When I received a draft of the agreement for review, they had drafted the agreement to the benefit of xpedx, which was expected. The interest rate was slightly above market rate, which was acceptable considering the business risk with no prepayment penalties. But the agreement required Hardy to purchase *all* packaging supplies from xpedx. I asked xpedx to provide a price list for all supplies that I was required to purchase before approving the agreement. The price list cost was 15 percent above our current supply costs. I asked to update the contract supply provision to state that our pricing would be equal to or lower than competitor pricing or Hardy could use our current vendors. During the term of the lease, Hardy made minimum purchases from xpedx and the deal worked out. But if I had signed on the dotted line without reading, our cost for all supplies would have increased by 15 percent and we would have paid dearly for that deal.

If It Looks Too Good to be True...

Typically, it is. The cost of a contract includes all costs above normal expenditures. In the case of our deal with xpedx, the cost was interest, fees, and penalty clauses. Additionally, the supply cost of 15 percent above market rate was part of the contract cost.

Payday loans, term loans, and credit card companies earn more on late fees and other fees than interest. Read the contract's fine print or the decision to sign on the dotted line could impact you for years afterward.

When I started Henderson Transloading, we started with a single contract. That first customer needed transloading services a year earlier than we predicted we would be ready. They offered the use of their equipment to get my business started, but the offer appeared too good to be true. And it was. The contract had provisions that could have placed my business at risk. They wanted an exclusive contract, which would prevent providing transloading services for other companies. As a third-party transloader, I needed the flexibility to work for anyone and everyone. An exclusive agreement should only be granted if the client purchases all of your business's capacity.

When I was a co-packer for Coca-Cola, the contract prohibited Hardy Bottling from contracting with Pepsi. In exchange for this provision, the contract had what is referred to as a "take or pay" provision. Coke paid for a minimum volume during the term of the contract as payment for this provision.

Going back to the situation with Henderson's first customer, when I raised my objection to the exclusivity provision, the customer said the exclusive provision was not important and they would not enforce it. They asked me to sign the contract as written. They said they would allow me to work for anyone; I just needed to let them know the customer's name. I told them I would not sign it as written; the contract had to represent the terms under which we would actually operate. Contracts are written to protect your family and any business owners who are not party to negotiations. I told them that if we could not remove those terms, I was not interested in the opportunity.

Eight months later, I received an offer from a major grain company. This company wanted me to start work in thirty days. I notified that first customer since it was their equipment my company was using. They immediately threatened to sue me for violating the contract. They sent email after email threatening to prosecute Henderson to the maximum extent of the law for not honoring the exclusive agreement. This went on for several weeks until I finally sent them a summary of our communications and the final signed agreement in which we removed the exclusivity agreement. The agreement signed by both parties did not contain exclusivity language. Thereafter, the tone of their communications changed. Remember, they claimed this would not be an issue when I originally asked them to change the language, and that is why I do not sign on the dotted line until the contract is correct. And I walk away if the other company will not correct it.

Contracts written by the seller are, of course, written to protect the seller. The buyer or owner's job is to protect the business. If I had not thoroughly read the contract with this first company, the terms and conditions would have destroyed my business. We avoided paying for services by reading and challenging the contract. Parties are not bound by terms not found in the contract. The contract should clearly state the buyer and seller's intentions to conduct business. As demonstrated, verbal commitments and promises do not count; put it in writing. Do not sign a contract under pressure, and, if possible, hire legal counsel.

A complete contract should address the full extent of the obligations of both the buyer and the seller. It is important to consider both the best-case scenario and worst-case scenario when writing a contract. All verbal promises or commitments during meetings must be reduced to writing in the contract. A contract can only cover what's included in writing, not what's promised or implied in informal conversations. It should cover pricing, specifications of the product or service, timeline, termination language, delivery method, buyer and seller responsibilities, confidentiality, and anything else that is important to your business. Take the time to thoroughly review all clauses, terms, and conditions. I always question any provision in the contract I do not understand or does not apply to me.

As a rule, if a clause is vague or is not applicable, I cross it out. It forces the seller to discuss the intent of clause. I have been told a provision is for "special conditions" or "pay no attention because we will never enforce it." If the clause doesn't apply to you, don't accept it in writing. Strike it and initial the change. Once you sign the contract, everything in the contract applies, regardless of anything that was said verbally. If this is not your strong point, hire a lawyer. Always get a copy of anything you sign and maintain proof of the contract.

I also advise you get to know with whom you are entering into an agreement. I do not do business with people I do not trust. There are not enough provisions in a contract to protect you from a dishonest person or business. A contract is business, and the contract must win every time. Thoroughly read the contract, including the fine print, before signing and never sign a blank contract. It is critical that you know your rights, do not sign under pressure, and include a termination clause that is good for both parties. A win-win contract also clearly outlines the obligations of both parties.

Attorneys

Many small businesses save on legal costs by not hiring an attorney. I have seen many contracts written by a business owner who has cut and pasted them from legal documents they either found online or through associates. This is a very dangerous practice that places your business at risk. How do you know whether the law has changed or whether the sources are credible or whether the documents you've put together are appropriate and/or complete?

If you make the wrong decisions or enter legal agreements that don't protect your interests, those actions will cost you many times more than a legal counsel would have. If you neglect to seek legal advice, the outcome could threaten the existence of your business.

We all understand that attorneys are expensive with prices ranging from 200 to 600 dollars per hour. Ask attorneys for references from businesses like your own. Check their references to evaluate other businesses' satisfaction with timeliness of service, quality of advice, and cost of service. Ask whether they believe the money spent on legal counsel was money well-spent. Attorneys who regularly counsel small businesses and startups understand their clients have limited budgets.

Experienced attorneys can save you time, aggravation, and money by providing the right advice at the right time. At a minimum, if the other party has a lawyer, I recommend you also hire a lawyer to level the playing field.

During my years as a business owner, there have been times when I have been desperate to gain new contracts to save my company. But during contract negotiations, I never allowed desperation to force me into making poor decisions. The automatic renewal for the copier taught me the hard way to thoroughly read all contracts. The basic rule is to ensure the contract provisions match your business needs. If provisions are not applicable to your business or unacceptable, remove them. Lastly, contract costs do not just include the interest, fees, and legal jargon. If you are required to pay above market rates for services or adhere to an exclusive arrangement, it's a cost. These hidden costs can often exceed the interest rate.

Signing on the dotted line may be your lifeline—or cause you to flatline; therefore, proceed with caution and care and read everything carefully before signing on the dotted line.

Based upon your reading about "Signing on the Dotted Line," what actions will you take? Suggestions:

List all contracts with the date the contract was signed and expiration dates. If a contract is over five years old, plan to rebid. It may save you money and improve services.

_____

_____

_____

Review all customer contracts. If you were in control, what provisions would you change? Draft a contract template with the new provisions for future opportunities.

_____

_____

_____

Meet with a contract attorney. The initial meeting is usually free. Review the contract template used for your business. Ask them how they can help you.

_____

_____

_____

Chapter 17:

Leading the Way

Edward R. Stettinius Jr., nineteenth century businessman, secretary of state, and Ambassador to the United Nations wrote, "We can achieve the utmost in economies by engineering knowledge, we can conquer new fields by research; we can build plants and machines that shall stand among the wonders of the world; but unless we put the right man in the right place—unless we make it possible for our workers and executives alike to enjoy a sense of satisfaction in their jobs, our efforts will have been in vain."

Coors Corporate Town Hall Meeting

I attended my first town hall meeting at Coors my fourth day on the job. I was introduced as the new vice president and general manager for the Memphis facility. Coors's CFO presented the company's financials and the COO presented its operation activities and performance. After the presentations, the meeting was opened for questions.

Employees appeared agitated, and the meeting had an air of anticipation. Coors and The Teamsters union that represented the hourly employees were negotiating a new three-year contract. Employees' tones were harsh, and emotions were high. Employees were not listening with interest but appeared to be waiting for the formal presentations to end. They were waiting for their turn to speak.

The first question was, "Why isn't Coors agreeing to the union wage and benefit proposal?"

The COO explained that the contract was negotiated between The Teamsters's and Coors's negotiation teams. He was confident that Coors's lead negotiator would be fair. When the employee went on to state that Coors did not listen to its employees' input and did not believe in the Memphis team, the COO responded that the Memphis benefits were equal to or higher than both Coors's other facilities and the industry average.

A few questions later, another employee walked up to the podium to use the microphone to ask a question. He returned to the back of room with the microphone, which allowed him to take control of the meeting. He asked the COO back-to-back questions, not waiting for a response to any of them. His goal was to anger employees. His final question was: "Why didn't Coors offer a better pension? Doesn't Coors care about employees who dedicate their life to the brewery?"

Never Let Them See You Sweat

The COO was clueless about controlling the audience, and he visibly hated confrontation. He had no poker face, appearing uneasy. This only made matters worse. My rule is to never let employees or customers see you sweat. People ask me whether

I get nervous during confrontations or when I have differing opinions from someone, and I don't. I have no reason to be nervous since a reply rarely kills anyone.

This Coors employee only controlled the conversation with the microphone for about ten minutes, but it felt like hours. Neither the employee's manager nor the human resource director intervened. I realized that management was not going to get the meeting under control, so I stood up. I offered to address the employee's pension questions. My voice was purposely low since my objective was to get the microphone. And I kept speaking in a very low voice as I walked over to the employee to retrieve the microphone.

Once I had the microphone, I explained to employees that the most recent manufacturing wage and benefits survey for the Memphis market included Coors. Based on this survey, Coors's pension benefits were one of the best in the Memphis region. I explained that the survey included DuPont, Kellogg, Coke, Pepsi, Cargill, and many others. They asked how I knew, and I explained I was a former human resource manager. It was my job to know this information.

When I finished answering their questions, I walked over to the COO and whispered, "Do not release this microphone again under any circumstances. Let them speak up and you repeat the questions for everyone to hear." I offered to address any questions applicable to Memphis since employees needed to become comfortable with my leadership style.

I wanted employees to understand they were not victims in this situation. Coors paid above-market wages and benefits, but the union had convinced some employees that their wages and benefits were not competitive, causing negative emotions. I shared the hourly wage rate of the other large manufactures in Memphis. These facts calmed the emotions of employees. Later, I learned that several employees' spouses worked for other companies in the survey and they confirmed the information I provided was accurate. This meeting was only my first, but right from the start it built employee confidence in my knowledge and leadership style.

One-on-one

After that first town hall meeting, my administrator made a list of all employees who voiced concerns. She documented each question next to the employee's name. I met with each employee on the list. I asked employees to provide details about their concerns. I asked why everyone seemed to have a negative tone. Employees were frustrated because management never followed up unless they showed anger. Employees effectively used anger and aggression to get management's attention. I told them it was now my job to address the plant's issues with the support of my leadership team. I made the commitment that my team would follow up in the future and let them know that anger was not required.

I communicated the results of my employee listening sessions to my management team. I shared that employees felt they did not have a voice. They lacked respect, trust, and confidence in management. They used the union grievance process and negotiations to level the playing field. I told my team these behaviors must change on both sides. This directive was not negotiable.

Employees were using the town hall meetings as a cry for help. Employees deserve leaders who are also employee advocates. A leader's primary role is helping employees achieve their personal best. Leaders must do as they say and say what they do in order to build trust. A 2007 study conducted by the Center of Creative Management found that 84 percent of business leaders believe that the definition of effective leadership is flexibility, collaborative skills, and the ability to create an environment that nurtures success.[12] So it seems the problem lies more with a leader's ability to translate this definition of leadership into everyday actions.

Inclusivity

The leadership characteristics included in the definition of leadership above are highly desirable for building a culture in which employees feel the company cares about their input and needs.

A company can provide great benefits like Coors but still fall short because of a lack of inclusiveness. Lack of inclusiveness causes employees to feel undervalued. Leaders can create a sense of transparency and build trust by engaging employees during town hall meetings, answering questions, and articulating those answers in layman's terms. It is important to answer employees' questions, whether good or bad. Surveys show that employees actually appreciate honesty and transparency over competitive wages.

During the Coors corporate town hall meeting, employees voicing local concerns indicated that the team did not trust their local management to answer their questions or keep their commitments.

Keeping commitments is the foundation of integrity and trust. Employees expect management to keep their word. If management promises action by a specific date, they need to keep that commitment. Management does not get a pass by making excuses such as meetings, too busy, traveling, preparing reports, etc.

Employees don't care about excuses. They just want to have confidence in leaders and trust them to keep their word.

Integrity is also linked to openness and honesty during interactions with employees. Similar to employee integrity, integrity for leaders requires them to take responsibility for mistakes instead of passing the blame or taking credit from a coworker. Integrity, in business and in life, means doing the right thing even when it is not easy or uncomfortable.

Managers can also improve employee morale and productivity by taking the time to understand what motivates their employees. Employees' actions at the town hall meeting were a cry for help. Therefore, a good starting point for me was talking to the employees who spoke during the meeting. They obviously had pressing issues that needed to be communicated. Managers could speak directly to each employee to understand what aspects of the job or the company were challenging. Employees needed many conversations to transition from anger to trust. The newfound relationship at Coors required management to continue to be an attentive listener and demonstrate to employees that they were truly interested in what they had to say.

In addition to individual conversations, managers were encouraged to include employees in team meetings and decisions impacting their areas. For example, we used safety meetings to open more dialogue. Afterward, the log of safety work orders was posted on all bulletin boards to demonstrate timely action and follow-up on employee concerns. Concern about safety communicates to employees that their managers and the company care.

Listening Tour

Whenever I start a new job or implement major change, my management style is to go on what I call a "listening tour." A listening tour is when management meets with as many key stakeholders as possible to ask questions, hear concerns, identify barriers, and build rapport. These tours provided valuable information from employees while ensuring all employees provided their input for concerns and changes. As leaders outline new expectations, listening tours ensure there is effective communication of any concerns or barriers that may impede the team's ability to accomplish the new goals. Leaders who speak freely with employees promote respect for leadership. An effective leader also follows through, which maintains emotional equity while providing feedback, and effective feedback throughout the year eliminates surprises.

Prior to the next town hall meeting with the CEO of Coors, I reviewed the names on the list from the first meeting. I knew these employees were not afraid to ask questions or speak up. But they needed coaching on how to ask questions in a way that would benefit other employees. I asked each one what they would like to know from the CEO. They were interested in a broad range of topics, and I encouraged each of them to ask questions. But I suggested they ask those questions in a tone similar to an exchange with a minister or friend. I coached them to use terms in their question that all employees understood and to allow time for other employees to ask questions. I wanted them to believe this was their meeting. This change demonstrated to management that leadership really could occur at every level of the organization if they allowed it to blossom. Leadership has very little to do with status or position.

Eventually, the management team began to notice the change in employee morale. They saw that follow-up caused employees to share other concerns and opportunities. They observed firsthand the benefit of building trust, following up, providing positive feedback, and giving recognition for good performance. Listening to employees and letting them know they are valued leads to an improved sense of self and job satisfaction, thereby inspiring employees to go above and beyond what is expected.

Inspiring New Ideas

One common frustration of business owners is a lack of new ideas. The rare employee who is innovative and creative is an asset. But idea people are generally not applauded. They frequently live at the edge of innovation in a separate universe and are treated as an outsider because people think they're weird. Personally, I love to surround myself with these personality types. I want to hear what they have to say since it's a leader's job to sift through ideas and decide which ones have merit. Also, I live for new ideas on how to build a better mousetrap.

Oliver Wendell Holmes wrote, "Many ideas grow better when transplanted into another mind than in the one where they sprang up." Your leadership style should build steps for employees to freely share ideas so they can achieve world-class results instead of wasting creativity and anger to get your attention. An engaged employee can take small creative nuggets and transform your company—if your leadership style promotes it.

Based upon your reading about "Leading the Way," what actions will you take? Suggestions:

Speak with employees about problems in their area and ask for ideas on how to solve them.

_____

_____

_____

List examples of how you have demonstrated your appreciation and respect for employees.

_____

_____

_____

How do you think your employees view your leadership style?
Why?

_____

_____

_____

Ask employees how they view your leadership style.

_____

_____

_____

Chapter 18:

The Right Role Models

Oprah Winfrey, famous actress, writer, TV personality, and businesswoman, wrote, "A mentor is someone who allows you to see the hope inside yourself. A mentor is someone who allows you to know that no matter how dark the night, in the morning, joy will come. A mentor is someone who allows you to see the higher part of yourself when sometimes it becomes hidden to your own view."

Oprah's quote certainly best summarizes my experience of being mentored.

Finding the Right Mentor

One of my mentors, Bob Morrison, former COO of Smucker's, was respected, knowledgeable, and influential, and he understood the priorities of the C-suite. Most importantly, he believed in me. During his forty-plus year tenure with Smucker's, he had mentored both the president and CEO of Smucker's. Therefore, he had their respect and ears at the time he was mentoring me.

Bob and I had many meetings to discuss my career aspirations after I graduated with my MBA. I told him that my future ambition was to become a plant manager at Smucker's. At the time, all plant managers were white males. But instead of telling me no, Bob explained the experience and leadership requirements. Then he said, "I think you will be great for this opportunity."

The first step toward my goal required me to learn operations management. As I mentioned in an earlier chapter, after Smucker's Memphis quality manager was transferred to the Orrville, Ohio office, I was offered the position of quality manager. Bob's mentoring was critical in guiding me through the experience requirements, providing exposure to the C-suite executives, and being my champion in closed-door board meetings. Based on his recommendation, I was offered the quality manager's position. I was told this role was a precursor to promotion to plant manager.

There were many others interested in the job who did not have Bob as a mentor and advocate. Bob knew that the quality manager position would demonstrate my ability to lead the facility by demonstrating my out-of-the-box thinking, leadership skills, and willingness to introduce innovation and world-class change.

Bob also knew I enjoyed my role as an accountant. Therefore, he was honest when telling me about the leadership characteristics and knowledge that I would need. We developed a training plan that was handled by the best quality manager in the company. That quality manager's advice was that success in operations would not occur from my office. He told me that great leaders perform listening tours every day, which some people call managing by walking around. I was to meet my people and listen to them at their place of work in their comfort zone. My success would be measured by my ability to connect and engage the employees who make the magic happen every day—the operators. As you climb the corporate ladder, active listening shows respect, and empowering my employees would only increase my capacity for success.

Two years after I was promoted to quality manager, Bob recommended my promotion to human resource manager and ultimately to plant manager. I will never forget his statement after the last promotion. As a plant manager, he said that my performance was based on the results of the entire facility. He said, "This is your team and your show. Therefore, run it like it is your company."

Bob's influence with and knowledge of the company guided me to become its first black and first female plant manager. As a mentee, it was critical for me to be open to his advice. He provided the guidance, but I had to put in the work.

A large part of our mentorship relationship was that we did not allow cultural differences or past experiences and norms to be roadblocks. There were times when I felt that my open desire to advance coupled with my passion, self-confidence, and energy provided personal satisfaction to my mentors. I know I changed Bob's perception of women and minorities. And having him as a mentor helped me understand that mentors do not have to look like you or come from the same background as you. He also helped me understand that others can and will respect and accept my differences. I am confident it was a refreshing experience for him as well.

Great Mentors

Anthony K. Tjan, entrepreneur and author, wrote an article in the *Harvard Business Review* entitled "What Great Mentors Do." In it, he says, "Too many mentors see mentoring as a training program focused around the acquisition of job skills. Obviously, one element of mentorship involves mastering the necessary competencies for a given position. But the best leaders go beyond competency, focusing on helping to shape other people's character, values, self-awareness, empathy, and capacity for respect. They know in the long run that there is a hard truth about soft matters and that these values-based qualities matter a lot more than skill enhancement. There are many ways to mentor people around these values and to build greater self-awareness."

Most people would tell you that they did not achieve their success alone. They can often point to someone who helped them along the way. This support typically takes the form of mentoring. I am fortunate to have benefited from several amazing mentors. My most effective business mentors were Bob Morrison, who I've already talked about, Dick Troyak, former plant manager and COO of the J. M. Smucker Company, and Dick Jirsa, CFO of Smucker's.

Mentors come from all walks of life. In my life, those men I listed provided guidance at the right time. I had many career aspirations that appeared out of my reach since, at the time, Smucker's lacked minorities or females in its C-suite. In an article titled "Mentoring, Organizational Rank, and Women's Perceptions of Advancement Opportunities in the Workplace," Christa Ellen Washington states that there are four critical career strategies for women to overcome career barriers and attain senior level positions:

1. Consistently exceed performance expectations.
2. Develop a style with which the company feels comfortable.
3. Seek out challenging and visible assignments.
4. Obtain the support of an influential mentor.[13]

Dick Troyak, as a mentor, taught me the importance of making the C-suite comfortable with a female black leader. As the first female in operations and the C-suite at Smucker's, this was a hurdle I had to overcome. He said that I had to own this problem if I wanted to grow within the company. I had to allow the Smucker family to get to know more about my family at every opportunity. Dick told me that the company promoted people they knew and were comfortable with, regardless of results. Like many others, I thought being smart and great at my job would lead me to success. He taught me that was only part of the requirement for promotion.

As a department manager, Dick provided opportunities to present the facility's performance to C-suite executives. I remember my first presentation about a sewer upgrade project. Before that presentation, I knew very little about sewer treatment. In preparation for the presentation, I asked Dick for help. I set up a recorder and scheduled a meeting with him in the conference room. When he arrived, I asked him to give the sewer facility upgrade presentation. After the presentation, I researched terms I did not understand. Then I developed my presentation, which I practiced with him. I had him ask questions similar to those my audience would ask.

I made the presentation to the CEO, C-suite, and quality managers. Thanks to Dick's help with preparation, I was able to answer all of their questions with confidence and clarity. After the presentation, the CEO stated that he was impressed with my operations knowledge.

At dinners with the CEO and other executives, Dick always ensured I was seated next to a different executive to allow each one to get to know me personally. As they became more comfortable with me, the range of topics expanded. After a few months, they began discussing business at the dinner table. Thereafter, I was invited to meetings with executives for ideation sessions.

The Council of Graduate Schools cites Morris Zelditch's summary of a mentor's multiple roles like this: "Mentors are advisors, people with career experience willing to share their knowledge; supporters, people who give emotional and moral encouragement; tutors, people who give specific feedback on one's performance; masters, in the sense of employers to whom one is apprenticed; sponsors, sources of information about and aid in obtaining opportunities; models, of identity and the kind of person one should be an academic."[14]

My mentors were great advisors who were willing to take the risk of accepting a black female as a mentee. As I grew within the company, Bob also provided greater opportunities and shared more confidence in me. I was the benefactor of an informal mentoring program by Smucker's executives.

My mentors filled a void in my knowledge and experience, which helped me achieve my ambition of becoming a plant manager. They were not threatened by my personal ambition and desire for promotion. Their inclusiveness started before the concept was embraced by Corporate America. And if men are willing to mentor women, I believe women must support the growth of other women. The willingness of these men to mentor me helped me become a better mentor to others.

Mentee to Mentor

My first mentoring opportunity came after I became a quality manager. After the promotion, I set a lofty goal to improve the performance of the department and hire women and minorities in the process. I was successful in getting a head count addition for a new quality supervisor. I hired a young college graduate named Bernadette who had the fundamental education in physical science and strong people skills, but she needed real life experiences. During the next ten years, I invested in her to help her achieve her personal best.

Bernadette's early challenges were helpful for her growth. One fond memory was her first encounter with a six-and-a-half-foot male supervisor who was ten years her senior in both age and experience. He had a reputation for bullying others with his massive size. Bernadette and I were both about 5'5" weighing 135 pounds wet. One day, she said, "He will not address quality issues with his team."

I instructed her to meet with him again and review the written list of issues. At the conclusion of the meeting, I told her to let him know that the quality manager would perform the follow-up inspection by the end of week. I encouraged her to let him know she was doing him a favor by giving him advance notice. If the issues were resolved, his department would stand out, or he would fall short by failing the audit. He was wrong in thinking that a failed audit impacted her performance instead of his department. Everyone knew that if the manager found the same problems, the outcome would not be good. The quality deviations were addressed prior to management's inspection, and the relationship between the two leaders grew to mutual respect.

Young leaders must have tools to be successful. They are expected to handle complex situations without much experience. My team understood I was on their team. Bernadette's communication of expectations placed ownership where it belonged. She made it easy for the supervisor to win, while remaining calm and professional. She tactfully left the monkey on his back and won the respect of her peers and employees. After this win, she had more skills and confidence to challenge other complex situations.

Years later, Bernadette was promoted to Smucker's quality manager at the largest jelly manufacturer in the world. I remember our discussion about her upcoming interview for the job. She was excited about the prospect of this opportunity. She asked, "What advice do you have for me? How do I gain the courage and boldness to address issues other managers avoid? How do I win this promotion?"

I told her, "You have already made a positive initial impression, which is why you are on the short list of candidates." During the interview, all she needed to do was close the deal. I told her to carry herself as if she were the quality manager by being confident and knowledgeable and looking the part. The key decision-makers had to visualize her in this position. Lastly, she had to educate interviewers about how her leadership skills and style would improve quality programming through greater employee empowerment and engagement.

How did she gain the courage and confidence to address complex issues while maintaining relationships? I call this not leaving dead bodies. Dead bodies occur during a conversation or interaction. Your attitude or mannerism toward the other party is so repulsive or such a turn off that the other party will do everything possible to avoid you. The concept of leaving dead bodies is discussed in detail in my first book, *Look Up*.

When addressing complex issues, I tell mentees to present the facts. I have a favorite quote: "In God we trust, all others bring data." In other words, always do your homework; find the facts. In meetings, be prepared to participate. You must establish a reputation for thoroughness, knowledge, and professionalism. Your goal is to create the best recommendation. There is no "I" and there is a lot of "we."

I asked Bernadette if this advice matched her experience with me over the years. She said it did. I told her, "Therefore, as you approach this new opportunity, ask, what would Carolyn say or do? Feel free to use my voice until you hear Bernadette's voice in the back of your head."

Preparation builds the confidence to participate while removing fear of making a fool of yourself. Bernadette had prepared for many meetings, and her input was valued and respected. She had built confidence while earning the respect of her peers. This was her story and her voice, and she needed to become comfortable reading from her own playbook.

Self-help books are big business. If you need to change a style or direction, these books give you simple recipes for success. Self-help books use the stories of others because it is easier to learn from others' experiences. Over time, most people adopt their own style. In the same vein, I encouraged her to be herself while leaning on her education, experiences, observations, and leadership skills. As a mentor, I was confident my mentee was ready to fly on her own.

The best mentor is a role model, counselor, and advisor who tells you the truth about your knowledge, skills, leadership, strengths, and weaknesses. They are willing to get to know you. A mentor has a heart for others and gains personal satisfaction from the accomplishments of others. They rarely seek recognition or personal gain, and they have your best interest at heart.

Winston Churchill, famous author and politician, said, "We make a living by what we get, we make a life by what we give."

Dick, Dick, and Bob saw potential in a young lady who rose from poverty to become CEO of her own companies. I had limited exposure to a broad range of professionals. My mentors lived up to Churchill's quote by measuring their lives by what they gave. I continue the journey by reaching back to help others in a similar manner.

Like my mentors, I gain personal satisfaction from the success of many mentees, which includes my three wonderful successful children: Jennifer, Whitney, and Christopher. I measure my success in life by the impact I have on others, by contributing to the next generation of mentors who can give back. In a perfect world, the mentee becomes the mentor and leaves the world an even better place. I had help in becoming the best version of my personal self. Remember, when you get a hand, give a hand.

Based upon your reading about "The Right Role Models," what actions will you take? Suggestions:

Make a list of those who mentored you.

_____

_____

_____

Make a list of how those mentors changed your life. Be specific, e.g., better delegator, public speaker, trusting others.

_____

_____

_____

Make a list of the people you mentored. What did you learn and where are they now?

_____

_____

_____

Review your list of employees or other young professionals. Who can you mentor? How will you get started?

_____

_____

_____

Chapter 19:

Overcompensating? No Such Thing

In 2018, the NFIB report entitled "Small Businesses Hiring or Trying to Hire Hits Nineteen Year High" states that business owners are continuing to plan for compensation increases as finding qualified workers remains one of the biggest problems for them. Small business owners are continuing to hire and create new jobs at historically high levels. "Small business owners, once again, are continuing to be the driving force of our economy by hiring at record levels and adding new jobs," said **NFIB president and CEO Juanita Duggan**. "The number of owners hiring or looking for workers strengthened."

"Small businesses are keeping the strong economic momentum going in the New Year," adds NFIB's chief economist Bill Dunkelberg. "They are adding jobs and raising compensation. With the help of tax and regulatory relief, the small business economy is a strong force."[15]

Compensation

Yet, for many growing organizations, it's a struggle to pay employees more while keeping their services and pricing competitive. "What owners can offer in wages depends on their ability to raise prices—and we haven't seen a big increase in prices," says Holly Wade, NFIB director of research.

Smaller companies typically can offer equal or higher pay than larger organizations but tend to fall short on benefits such as healthcare, profit sharing, and company stock. Even with equal or higher pay, 60 percent of smaller companies report hiring or trying to hire, but 88 percent of those report few or no qualified applicants.[16]

I needed managers and skilled operators when I started Hardy Bottling. The facility was 1.3 million square feet with complex processes and systems. In order to jump-start the operation, the new team had to understand the facility, systems, business processes, and people. Hiring the right people was the difference between success and failure for my new company.

Hardy Bottling's key managers were hired from Smucker's and Coors. I hired mentees and/or employees whose promotions I had influenced. Early in their careers, I recognized their leadership and technical abilities. They deserved opportunities for advancement through training and assignment to corporate projects. As I talked about in terms in mentorship, my leadership style includes investing in my employees. I do not expect a personal return from employees other than their loyalty and dedication to the company. In this case, they were loyal to me; therefore, they were willing to make personal sacrifices to join me at Hardy Bottling.

A Shared Dream

When I opened Hardy Bottling, I offered my new leaders the same salary they earned at their previous job plus healthcare. My top executives were also offered a major payout if the company was later sold. I committed to a minimum payout, which I worked to exceed. Their confidence in my ability and their loyalty to me caused them to bet on our success. I could not offer a 401K or other benefits. But I offered hopes and dreams. They were confident Hardy Bottling would win and that they would share in the upside. Therefore, everyone adopted my personal ambitions and dreams.

Another challenge for small businesses is hiring initial staff on a part-time rather than full-time schedule. Employees' personal financial situation typically requires a forty-hour workweek, so sometimes small businesses must offer a fixed payment of forty hours per week regardless of the actual work schedule. If a company has limited working capital, this option typically is not financially feasible, so the next option would be to hire fewer employees but to make sure those you do hire are multi-skill employees. Employees with multiple skills can be assigned to different tasks in order to work forty hours per week.

Every business needs an account payables clerk. After Hardy's account payable clerk quit, we realized we only needed this clerk one day a week instead of five. An employee recommended a friend who was an account payables clerk for another company. He thought the friend would agree to work one day a week as a contractor. We hired him to work eight hours each Saturday processing account payables for us. This saved us thirty-two hours a week without compromising the quality of work, which was a great way for a growing business to save money. When our accounting needs grew and we could afford a full-time clerk, we hired the same accounting clerk as a full-time employee.

Technology

Another solution that can make your money go further is using technology to improve the efficiency of the workforce. When you increase efficiency, you can hire fewer employees. Hiring fewer employees allows business owners to pay higher wages. When we started Henderson Transloading, fifteen employees loaded fifteen containers of grains in a sixteen-hour day. We built a new transloading facility and developed custom software for it. This new system loads eight loads per hour with five employees. Technology allowed us to hire fewer people, which increased our efficiency and allowed us to pay those few people higher wages.

Loyalty

An intangible benefit for Hardy's employees was a higher feeling of self-worth, autonomy, and self-direction. Employee input was expected and respected, and Hardy offered a better lifestyle, more flexibility, and a sense of pride. We paid employees comparable wages even though we had fewer benefits. Unlike large companies, our personnel policies considered the needs of employees, such as flexible work schedules, overtime assignments, transportation home or to work, or an office worker bringing their child to work if no sitter was available.

Hardy's employees also worked first shift, which is rare in manufacturing.

At one point, another company recruited several of our employees, but that company's work schedule rotated from day to night on a regular basis. Many employees returned to Hardy because our day shift (first shift) gave them a life. Also, they missed the autonomy and respect for their contribution.

One rule we had was that employees who left a second time were not eligible for rehire. We realized that people make mistakes and sometimes leave their job on a whim. We were committed to our employees and needed them to commit to us in return. Leaving twice is not a whim; it's a habit. Hardy required a stable workforce and could not deliver consistent quality of service with high turnover.

Amazingly, we won the loyalty of most hourly workers, but hiring professionals remained a challenge. All small businesses face similar challenges in hiring professional employees. Companies in need of specific skills must look for creative solutions. I once hired a controller who had retired from a car manufacturer. After six months of retirement, he was bored and missed his routine.

Age has Advantages

As I mentioned in a previous chapter, the advantage of hiring retired employees is their willingness to do a broader range of tasks using their broader range of skills. Retirees typically want a flexible schedule, respect, and part-time work. This fits perfectly with the small business part-time needs until that business grows. One of the best resources for finding retirees is Meritan or a similar organization. Meritan's website says they provide seniors employment and a job training program with community service.[17] Meritan provides on-the-job training for low-income, unemployed seniors over the age of fifty-five. This program is designed to help those who want to enter or re-enter the workforce. Participants benefit from free career services that help them find permanent job placements once their training is complete. I hired a retired plant controller, accounting clerk, operations manager, and delivery driver from Meritan. In addition to having a variety of job skills and being reliable, they are grateful for the job.

Respect Matters

A survey by Georgetown University's Christine Porath asked workers what matters most to them. Feeling respected by superiors often topped the list in their responses. They surveyed nearly 20,000 employees worldwide, and across the globe, respondents ranked respect as the most important leadership behavior. Yet, employees report more disrespectful and uncivil behavior each year.18 Employees who feel respected are more grateful for—and loyal to—their companies.

After five years, we decided to sell Hardy Bottling. The leaders received a payout significantly larger than I originally offered when hiring them. And they deserved every dollar. At Hardy, leaders worked tirelessly to accomplish the goals of the company. They performed mediocre tasks that most other leaders would have thought was beneath them, such as cutting grass and waxing floors to protect our image as a company. They worked long hours to manufacture and ship products to deliver world-class customer service.

The most exceptional results of my career came from my employees' commitment to winning. The team did whatever was necessary to satisfy customers. For example, we passed audits other co-packers could not because of our exceptional quality manager from Smucker's who was my VP of operations. Or, in another example, a customer needed the FRS product after we shut down for Thanksgiving. My team resumed work to ship the product and ensure delivery for Thanksgiving. The team demonstrated that everyday customer service was the norm, not the exception, and the payout from that sale was their reward.

My employees were valued and respected, and they respected the company in return. We promoted many employees to their first management positions when other companies would never have given them a chance because of their lack of management experience. When employees resigned and returned, the majority never left again. We understood that the value of employee engagement and labor relations at Hardy could not be replaced by better benefits from larger companies. We demonstrated our respect for employees through our actions, which included listening to and acting on employee input, ideas, and suggestions. Employees' contributions to the business were invaluable to our success. In return for our respect, employees also respected and valued customers.

Overcompensation can be both financial and cultural, allowing small businesses to compete while providing greater returns to their employees in a host of different ways. By far, the greatest return for employees is respect for their contributions and ideas, and that value is priceless.

Based upon your reading about "Overcompensating? No Such Thing," what actions will you take? Suggestions:

Make a list of employees you cannot afford to lose. Summarize why you think your employees work for you. Why do they prefer your company to other employers with better wages or benefits? This will help refine your message to attract new talent. Review their compensations. What bonuses or pay for performance ideas can you offer?

_____

_____

_____

How does your compensation program compare to competitors? List any differences.

_____

_____

_____

Make a list of non-monetary benefits you offer that set you apart. Make a list of employees' interests. How can you impact those?

_____

_____

_____

Chapter 20:

Everybody Wins

From the time I was seven to about ten years old, every day during the summer I would play marbles with my friends in the neighborhood. We would meet at the same place on the tiny walkway between houses in the dirt. The ideal play area was a flat dirt surface with shade. I always played to win. My goal was to win every game and collect all the marbles. Over time, I became the best marble shooter, winning all the games. But as time went on, I started finding my friends playing without me. And it hurt my feelings.

What is Winning

This experience taught me that no one likes to play with someone who wins all the time. Friends, family, and associates must believe they have a chance of winning in order to want to play. My friends did not feel like they could win against me at marbles, so to level the playing field, I was excluded.

So, I came up with a new strategy. I found my friends in their new location playing marbles. I stood there holding my jar of marbles and said, "I want to play." They looked pretty guilty for being caught hiding. On that day, I lost my first game. Amazingly, everyone was excited and suddenly became my friend again. I went home happy, leaving my friends feeling like they could win against me.

The truth is ... I lost on purpose. I had to accept that it was okay for me to win the majority of the time, but not all the time. I learned early in life that friendship was more important than winning every game. And really, winning is gaining what is important to you. Malcolm Forbes said it best, "If you've had a good time playing the game you're a winner even if you lose."

In business, the goal is to create outcomes in which everyone wins. This is only possible if each party is willing to give something up. We do not live in an all-or-nothing world. If you get the most important part of what you want, count it as a win. I have applied this philosophy in marriage, friendship, leadership, and business transactions. As result, people view me as selfless leader. They are attracted to me versus excluding me from their lives, just like my friends playing marbles.

Windfall

After my first year at Coors, I recommended downsizing the number of employees at the Memphis facility. If downsizing is mismanaged, the company loses employee confidence and years of valuable experience. My analysis of the employee demographics found that 20 percent of the workforce was eligible for a full union pension. Another 20 percent was eligible for both a union pension and social security. My goal was to provide financially tempting incentives to persuade employees to retire, while the union contract required junior employees to be forced out with senior employees retaining the jobs.

Typically, within a few years of younger workers securing new jobs, older workers retire. And employees who receive a windfall—an unexpected gain in income from receiving a severance, insurance payout, winning the lottery, unforeseen inheritance, etc.—tend to celebrate. But forced downsizing without any windfall leaves an emotional scar and distrust in the company. This distrust also impacts the performance of the employees remaining on the job. The real cost of mishandling downsizing is a loss of morale and productivity that costs millions of dollars. Watching a poorly handled downsizing, employees tend to believe their turn is coming; it's only a matter of time.

At Coors, we wanted employees to voluntarily apply for downsizing and view it as an opportunity to earn a windfall. My goal was to eliminate the need for forced termination. People should not be used and thrown away. They are your most valuable investment, which is why they are called human capital. It is management's responsibility to find creative ways for everybody to win. It's not cheap or free, but the positive impact on employee morale and confidence will be measured in efficiency, years of service, and low turnover.

Transparency and Understanding

In order to minimize the impact of downsizing on operational efficiency, we communicated regularly with both employees and their families. After those communications, we provided written copies to all employees, as well as mailed the documents to their homes. We held one-on-one meetings with employees and family members who didn't understand the offer. People do not trust what they do not understand, and it was management's job to help everyone understand the offering.

Prior to the downsizing offer, we also reorganized jobs and trained employees to handle new tasks. Packaging lines were reengineered to model world-class installations. The equipment re-engineering cost three million dollars, but it provided employees and the business the tools to make a successful change. The changes reduced head count and overtime and eliminated temporary employees. As a business, we had to get ready for the downsizing or it would have failed. The requirement to re-engineer the business prior to downsizing is missed by many organizations, resulting in them just rehiring the eliminated positions because they weren't prepared for the changes.

Compassion

Companies must also prepare upper management for the downsizing process. Managers need training to deal with the emotional and operational impact of the change. Untrained managers will complain that employees do not want to work and have a bad attitude after an announced downsizing, but they need to understand the employees' perspectives. The employee's life and identity is built around the company. This includes their community, quality of life, children's education, and retirement. The company's story is their story, and the company just changed the employee's narrative with limited notice. Compassion on the part of management is critical.

Again, remember not to judge employees' attitudes during this transition as they are driven by fear and the need to survive.

For example, after a downsizing announcement, managers might encounter employees who have a good attitude. Realistically, the employee is hoping his positive disposition will secure his position. On the other hand, another employee might be labeled as a troublemaker with a bad attitude. Clearly, the employee was never good at hiding their emotions. Therefore, the emotional reaction is heightened by fear, which is normal.

The downsizing at Coors ended up being a huge success. The company achieved the desired results, and only hourly employees applying for the windfall jobs were eliminated. We reduced head count, reorganized the operation to improve efficiency and safety, and maintained employee trust. Prior to the downsizing, our performance came in last of the three facilities. This change reduced our cost and improved our performance to be second out of the three. I shared this win with employees with greater quarterly bonuses.

Getting employees involved in downsizing and operations improvement efforts is critical. We held team meetings and town halls, which were intense, emotional, and time-consuming. This was not fun, but it was the right thing to do. I am not saying everyone was happy; however, the majority were happy with the severance and changes to the operations. I was once told you cannot please 100 percent of the people. There are a few people who you could give the keys to the building and they still would not be happy!

One of the biggest problems in downsizing comes from companies announcing reductions in force without adequate details. A company might be happy with the prospect of improved earnings and the press release plays up the long-term financial impact. But few press releases are written to meet the needs of employees and their families. The attorneys approving press releases are usually more concerned with the legal ramifications rather than employees' personal lives. A 10 percent reduction in force means that 10 percent of employees will no longer have insurance or a paycheck to meet their personal obligations. These employees are wondering how they are going to protect their family. They need answers that apply to their lives. Employees must be prepared to communicate with their family and friends after the press release, and for that to happen, they must understand the downsizing fully and in detail.

Win-Win

It is possible for everybody to win. Business must be willing to work to achieve the goals of all parties, and that allows everybody to win. The key is to put out inclusive communications while understanding what is important to all parties. All parties must also be willing to give a little, to compromise. Happy employees who are engaged and enjoy coming to work every day tend to work harder and care more about the company. Many people work hard behind-the-scenes to create little victories, such as covering for a sick employee or last-minute schedule changes or a last-minute delivery to a customer. These wins are just as important to the culture of your business as signing a major contract.

Remember, pride comes before the fall, transparency is the cousin of honesty, and happy employees are good for business and necessary to create a win-win. If you are good to your employees, they will be good to your customers; therefore, everybody wins.

Based upon your reading about "Everybody Wins," what actions will you take? Suggestions:

Make a list of recent communications about your business. How will you share any wins with employees? They key is to communicate employees' roles in the success.

_____

_____

_____

List the last three wins management celebrated with employees. Okay, list the three you *should have* celebrated.

_____

_____

_____

Make a list of tasks where employees went the extra mile. Did you thank them for their actions?

_____

_____

_____

Conclusion

Reflecting on my years as a business owner, there were certainly a lot of long days with some longer than others. But I love business ownership. The lives I touch, the families for which I am responsible, energize me with a sense of pride. Employees who previously earned minimum wage now earn a living wage working for my company and can feed their families.

I am making an impact on my community.

I hope I am changing people's lives.

As a business owner, I also love the adrenaline rush associated with winning. I enjoy solving a problem using my team's abilities and experiences to find creative solutions. Business owners say that business ownership will either keep you young or make you old. My business keeps my mind young. The key to successful business ownership is doing business for the right reasons. There is no greater satisfaction than seeing ideas you imagined grow and go on to impact others' lives.

In writing *Step Out*, I achieved another personal goal of sharing my life experiences through stories about my ups and downs. I want to be a mentor to the masses. One mentee at a time would take a lifetime and *Step Out* makes mass mentoring possible. My first business mentors were members of the chamber of commerce and several local CEOs, and their guidance was vital in avoiding landmines that could have derailed my business. Hopefully my discussion of mentors and mentees will inspire you to help others to fill this void as well.

When I launched my first business, I defined success as developing human capital and business growth. This was achieved through relationships with major brands that viewed our company, Hardy Bottling, as the home of their brands. We worked for over forty brands from big names to little-known businesses. My team understood that every customer was number one, regardless of size. Remember, there is power in people and relationships when everybody wins and understands the truth about opportunities.

The suggested actions at the end of the chapters will help your business become the next big thing. I challenge you to get started by following Walt Disney's advice: "First think, second dream, third believe and finally dare."

Many new businesses start in the owner's garage, at their kitchen table, or in a home office with a single employee, the owner. Growth brings complications because the business owner is always focused on servicing the new customer. Lack of business best practices and processes becomes an issue overnight after a problem pops up. Learn from the mistakes and stories of others and create your own processes to avoid many issues and identify problem early to minimize damage. Growth is the best way to identify weak business processes. This will not kill you, but it might hurt your pride and pocketbook. Remember, what does not kill you will make you stronger.

So, what should you do now?

Get started.

Summarize your responses to the suggested actions and questions at the end of each chapter. Prioritize your actions based on which will have the greatest impact on your business. Also, use a SWOT analysis to prioritize activities that address business threats and weaknesses.

I have led many business turnarounds in my career, and nothing gets the team excited like an early win. Find simple actions such as joining your local chamber of commerce or sending several team members to attend a lunch-and-learn to network. Immediate action communicates your commitment to change, and it starts now. You do not have all the time in the world, and it is true that the early bird gets the worm.

The greatest joy of business ownership is that you get to decide to build the company of your grandfather's day that values people as its greatest assets and responsibility. I run my businesses according to the quote from Thomas Watson Sr., former CEO of IBM, who said, "To be successful, you have to have your heart in your business, and your business in your heart."

Business owners have business in their hearts. They simply need processes to guide the business toward its desired outcomes. Tommy Hilfiger, famous designer, said, "The road to success is not easy to navigate, but with hard work, drive, and passion, it's possible to achieve the American dream." Your American dream has already started. *Step Out* is your tool to craft your story with a happy ending. Remember, don't take yourself too seriously. Mistakes will not kill; they will make you smarter the next time.

Thank you for reading *Step Out* and congratulations for daring to pursue the American dream.

Acknowledgments

I would like to extend my heartfelt appreciation to the many people who believed in me from early childhood through adulthood. I am forever grateful for the sacrifices and open hearts of others. These life experiences provided the materials and knowledge to make this publication possible.

My deepest love and thanks goes to my mother. She led by example during a war against poverty. Every day she led a family of sixteen into battle to fight a good fight with valor and grace. At no point did she complain or blame anyone for our situation. She felt that whining and complaining were a waste of time and energy. She focused on surviving to fight another day. Failure was never an option, and success was simple. Her kids, armed with food, clothes, and shelter, went off to school to gain the skills to win the war against poverty. She taught her team to develop a plan, focus on the goal, expect that sacrifices are normal, and work harder than the competition. Thank you, Mom, for this amazing foundation. Any time life looks impossible, I think about your resilience. I realize my obstacles fade when compared to your challenges. You refused to allow us to be a statistic. My life is dedicated to continuing your journey.

Great life experiences involve an amazing team. The great people who love me the most include my amazing husband,

Marino, and my three children, Jennifer, Whitney, and Christopher. My family had a front-row seat and walked beside me during my journey's ups and downs. My life experiences did not happen without a cost. My family's willingness to support new ideas and attack obstacles helped keep me sane. My home and family are my sanctuary, where I am the best version of myself. Thank you for being my rock and partners as I find the next mountain to climb.

Thanks to my siblings for helping with time management during my career. Being confident that you had my back for childcare allowed me to challenge life. Also, thanks to my brother and sister for believing in me enough to invest in my college education. This education created a solid foundation for my life.

The mentors in my life deserve a lifetime achievement award. Bob Morrison, Dick Jirsa, and Dick Troyak were my informal mentors. Their unselfish guidance and willingness to challenge the status quo by including a black female allowed me to be bold and creative and implement world-class change. I was fearless in implementing new ideas because you guys had my back. You supported me regardless of the risk to your career. These experiences taught me to help others achieve their personal best.

My life is full of blessings but one that I hold close to my heart is Deanie Parker. Thank you to Deanie, my friend, champion and confidant. Her support during my darkest days was critical to my survival. If she did not know the answer, she freely offered her vast village of connections. Deanie climbed the highest mountain to insure my success with no strings attached. She is not only my friend but will always be my guardian angel. Thank you to David Hancock, Morgan James CEO and Founder for believing in me to bring this work to life. Also, thank you to the Morgan James team of highly qualified professionals whose knowledge filled in gaps while guiding me using a highly efficient process. A special thanks to my Author Relations Manager, Bonnie Rauch for making the process seamless and easy. My other publishing heros and sheros include Jim Howard, Bethany Marshall, and Nickcole Watkins. David has built a team most organizations work a lifetime to achieve 'best in class'. Step Out demonstrates Morgan James publishing greatness.

In closing, Herbert A. Simon, a Jewish-American economist, political scientist, and cognitive psychologist, wrote, "The choices we make lead up to actual experiences. It is one thing to decide to climb a mountain. It is quite another to be on top of it." This quote sums up my life. Statistics say a person from poverty has a low probability of getting out. They dream, plan, and talk about a brighter future. In my life, I let my actions rather than my words demonstrate my achievements. My goal is to defy the odds. My word is my bond since I always walk the talk. My choices have led to experiences that allowed me to climb mountains and reach the top. Thank you for supporting me from the bottom to the mountaintop to create the experiences shared in *Step Out*. My American dream would not be possible without you.

Carolyn Chism Hardy

Moving Mountains and Needles

Carolyn Chism Hardy is taking women and minority business by storm. She is a fearless innovator of change, moving forward in commercial real estate development and as a distributor, exporter, author, and philanthropist. She is a trailblazer whose accomplishments in non-traditional jobs, business triumphs, and entrepreneurial achievements are unequalled by women and Blacks. Hardy operates on the forefront of business evolution as she uses innovation, creative ideas, and networks to roll out the next generation of ideas.

Carolyn began her career at the J. M. Smucker Company, successfully managing the finance, quality, and human resources departments before becoming the first African American female plant manager. After a successful career at Smucker's, she served as vice president of services at Honeywell-POMS Corporation where she was responsible for domestic and international software implementation. She then joined Coors Brewing Company and became the first African American female vice president and general manager of a major brewery.

As the founder and CEO of Chism Hardy Investments, Hardy is a job creator, innovator, and philanthropist. A passionate and determined investor, she purchased a former Coors Brewery in 2006 and started Hardy Bottling Company, which she sold in 2011. In 2012, she stepped up her investment in the neighborhood where she had worked her entire career. She invested over five million dollars building a new grain system to export grain and expanding her commercial leasing holdings. This grain expansion with her daughters, Jennifer and Whitney, leveraged the Memphis location to create jobs in a sector that is not only right for Memphis, but is also great for farmers in Tennessee, Arkansas, and Mississippi. Her vision: to build a unique Memphis-based supply chain management company. Her pathway: strong partnerships, proper capitalization, and first-to-market solutions. "I want to be the proof women and minorities have the skills and ability to build a significant company while demonstrating that women- and minority-owned businesses can compete," she says.

Her words of guidance: "Test your boundaries. Test your resilience. Test your capacity. Be the best version of yourself, and connect with your audiences." As an experienced businessperson, insignificant challenges and temporary obstacles seldom distract her. Hardy stays focused and keeps on pushing regardless of the size of the mountain. As a published author, her goal is to reach a broader audience to teach others how she's managed to move mountains.

A devoted philanthropist, Hardy is a founding member of Philanthropic Black Women and a board member of Federal Reserve of St. Louis, Tennessee Lottery, Tennessee Leadership Business Council, Methodist Le Bonheur Hospital, Greater Memphis Chamber, SCORE, and many others. Her vision is to build a vibrant community that is inclusive to increase prosperity for all.

Carolyn is engaged in Memphis's "rebirth" and industry growth through her support of the growth in skilled manufacturing jobs. As one of the founders of Southwest Industrial Readiness program, thousands of unemployed and underemployed Memphians have been trained and have secured jobs that pay a living wage and include benefits. Carolyn's primary objective is to support a greater Memphis by promoting growth and prosperity for all people.

"Every time the needle moves in Memphis, I work to ensure the needle moves for others," she says. Those "others" are small business, young entrepreneurs, business professionals, or economic development efforts that attract jobs and decrease poverty.

In 2019, Carolyn was named the first female Distinguished Citizen of Year for the Chickasaw Boy Scouts Council. She was inducted into the Society of Entrepreneurs in 2016 and into the African American Hall of Fame in 2010. She received the 2016 Dr. Martin Luther King Legacy Award, the 2016 River City Links National Trends and Services Award, the 2014 Ruby Wharton Award for Business, the 2013 Legends

Award from the Women's Foundation, and the 2012 Women of Achievement Award for Determination. In 2012, she was named as one of the 100 Women Who Inspired the Century by the University of Memphis Center for Women and African American Studies. She was also named 2012 Super Women in Business, 2011 University of Memphis Alumnus of the Year, and in 2009, Black Business Association named her business the Outstanding Woman-Owned Business and Business of the Year in 2008. These are only a few of the awards with which she and her businesses have been honored over the years.

Carolyn is married to Marino Hardy, and they are the proud parents of three wonderful children, Jennifer, Whitney, and Christopher.

Endnotes

1   Sawhill, Isabel V. "Still the Land of Opportunity?" Brookings. Brookings, May 10, 2017. https://www.brookings.edu/articles/still-the-land-of-opportunity/.

2   "Business Networking." Wikipedia. Wikimedia Foundation, December 9, 2019. https://en.wikipedia.org/wiki/Business_networking.

3   "About." Epicenter. Accessed February 27, 2020. https://www.epicentermemphis.org/about.

4   "Programs and Resources." Epicenter. Accessed February 27, 2020. https://www.epicentermemphis.org/resources.

5   Schooley, Skye. "SWOT Analysis: What It Is and When to Use It." Business News Daily. Business News Daily, June 24, 2019. https://www.businessnewsdaily.com/4245-swot-analysis.html.

6   Nolo. "Small Claims Court and Business Disputes." www.nolo.com. Nolo, June 13, 2012. https://www.nolo.com/legal-encyclopedia/small-claims-court-business-disputes-29568.html.

7   Diamantides, Alyse, "Creative Salem: A Public Relations Report." 2018. Honors Theses. 171. https://digitalcommons.salemstate.edu/honors_theses/171

8   Council, Young Entrepreneur. "Avoid These 4 Big Reasons Small Businesses Fail." Inc.com. Inc., June 28, 2019. https://www.inc.com/young-entrepreneur-council/avoid-these-4-big-reasons-small-businesses-fail.html.

9   Duke, Catherine. "The Most Common Payroll Mistakes Small Businesses Make." ScaleFactor. ScaleFactor, Inc., July 30, 2019. https://scalefactor.com/scaleblog/the-most-common-payroll-mistakes-small-businesses-make/.

10   Jacobsen, Darcy. "The Dangers of Employee Silence." Workhuman. Workhuman, February 16, 2020. https://www.workhuman.com/resources/globoforce-blog/the-dangers-of-employee-silence.

11   Steele, Chandra. "Outdated Technology in the Workplace Costs Companies." PCMAG. PCMag, November 6, 2019. https://www.pcmag.com/news/outdated-technology-in-the-workplace-costs-companies.

12   Dorward, Lisa. "Employee Expectations of an Effective Leader." Chron.com, November 21, 2017. https://work.chron.com/employee-expectations-effective-leader-3158.html.

13   Washington, Christa Ellen. "Mentoring, Organizational Rank, and Women's Perceptions of Advancement Opportunities in the Workplace." Forum on Public Policy, 2010. https://files.eric.ed.gov/fulltext/EJ903579.pdf.

14   *Adviser, Teacher, Role Model, Friend: on Being a Mentor to Students in Science and Engineering.* Washington, D.C: The National Academies Press, 1997. https://www.nap.edu/read/5789/chapter/2.

15   "Small Businesses Hiring or Trying to Hire Hits Nineteen Year High in NFIB June Jobs Report." NFIB.

National Federation of Independent Business, July 5, 2018. https://www.nfib.com/content/press-release/economy/small-businesses-hiring-or-trying-to-hire-hits-nineteen-year-high-in-nfib-june-jobs-report/.

16 "Small Businesses Struggling to Find Qualified Workers, Adding to October Growth Problem." NFIB. National Federation for Independent Business, October 31, 2019. https://www.nfib.com/content/press-release/economy/small-businesses-struggling-to-find-qualified-workers-adding-to-october-growth-problem/.

17 "Meritan." Meritan. Accessed February 27, 2020. https://meritan.org/.

18 Kristie Rogers. "Do Your Employees Feel Respected?" Harvard Business Review. Harvard Business Publishing, June 21, 2018. https://hbr.org/2018/07/do-your-employees-feel-respected.

If you've enjoyed *Step Out*, Carolyn Chism Hardy is the author of two other amazing books. Please take a minute to read this brief introduction to each book. They will provide great advice to guide you on your journey to achieve the life you deserve.

Good Luck!

Look Up
Five Principles of Intentional Leadership
Carolyn Chism Hardy

Writing *Look Up* was a labor of love. *Look Up* was my first book, which has received rave reviews from readers who attest to the value of its advice.

Notes are my companions. I write them all the time. When I have something I want to research further, I hear an interesting quote or I have an idea for a new business deal, I open my notepad and start writing. Over the years, I have filled thousands of pages with lessons learned and great ideas. Although I graduated from college years ago, these notes are a record of my continued education. I have been on a lifelong odyssey of growth and discovery. This book is a peek into my journey.

There is inherent value in learning from the path another has taken. These notes are the foundation for the guidance offered in this book. You hold in your hands a collection of golden nuggets of knowledge I learned along the way. Many were taught to me by mentors like my mother; Dick Jirsa, former CFO of Smucker's; Bob Morrison, the COO of Smucker's;

and countless others. I learned many other lessons the hard way through trial and error.

Leaders are like lighthouses. They are aware people look up to them for guidance. They light the way so others may reach their destination safely. Leaders offer guidance to buffer those who come after them. They keep them from hitting the rocks that are surely on their paths. They stand firm in their position and confident in their actions. This book will help you navigate away from the rocks and steer you into calmer waters.

The five principles in *Look Up* will be your lighthouse. The first principle is, "Plan Your Destiny" which helps the reader explore Know Your Why, Balance, and Don't Eat Excuses for Breakfast. The second principle is, "Make the Right Impression" which explores Know Your Worth, Stand Out, and Don't Let Bad News Age. The third principle is "Build Relationships" which discusses Understand Personalities, Don't Leave Dead Bodies and Never Let a Good Problem Go to Waste. The fourth principle is "Be the Change You Wish to See", which takes you through a journey of Use Your Education & Lean on Common Sense, Be Transparent and Become the Pro. The fifth principle is "Keep Calm and Carry On" which shares with the reader how to Be Prepared, Lead by Example and Always Pursue Growth.

Many people choose to ignore great advice. Some want to figure things out on their own. It's a lonely road for those who believe they don't need help. Those who can't master the principles in this book may never reach their destination.

During my career, discrimination towards my race and gender was commonplace. I had to endure prejudices that were unjust and unfair while maintaining my composure and work ethic. Overcoming obstacles that seemed insurmountable was critical to my success. I persevered because others who went before me showed me it was possible.

A great leader knows someone is always looking to them to be a role model, to motivate and lead the way. A French philosopher, Bernard of Chartres, once said, "We stand on the shoulders of giants." Almost 900 years later, his words still stand true. I stood on the shoulders of my mother. She passed along her wisdom and enabled me to benefit from the life she lived. I hope to do the same for you.

I hope anyone interested in rising to the challenge of leadership or entrepreneurialism will find guidance in the lessons I learned and the notes I took along the way.

Read this book, master the principles and remember to always, "Look Up." You are one of the giants on which the future depends.

The Impossible Turned Possible
Carolyn Chism Hardy

The Impossible Turned Possible is Carolyn's third book. It is a simple roadmap to guide, inspire and challenge you to achieve personal goals. This is the 'kick in the pants' many need to get started. The real-life stories were selected as examples of goals that most Americans desire to achieve.

The 5-step goal process follows the KISS theory, which means 'keeps it simple' to allow readers to understand, internalizes then execute. Setting big, lofty goals using the five-step plan will help you defy odds that were about as out of reach as placing a man on the moon over fifty years ago. Carolyn understands that dreaming is free, but achievement requires setting goals and developing a plan. Few goals are bigger than landing a man on the moon, which was viewed as impossible by many over fifty years ago.

The Impossible Turned Possible will motive and inspire you to take this first step on your journey to achieve the life you deserve.

The first step toward change is always the hardest. We find comfort in normalcy. And the bigger the change, the harder the first step. We are frightened by not knowing the outcome of change. We doubt ourselves, and we overthink the change. Sustainable change requires behavior change as the first step.

How can you reduce the power that fear has over you? *The Impossible Turned Possible* begins your personal transformation by transforming your attitude about change and winning.

The only failure in life is not trying. It is amazing how many people talk themselves out of greatness. They have a brilliant idea, but they quickly convince themselves, "It will never work." Amazingly, people give fear of failure more power than the rewards of success. So be the change you wish to see. Now is the time to change your impossible goals to possible.

Good luck!

CPSIA information can be obtained
at www.ICGtesting.com
Printed in the USA
JSHW021817060121
10754JS00001B/44